Table of Contents

**Jobs and Responsibilities
in the Tourism Industry**

Jobs and Responsibilities in the Tourism Industry

Goals

- Your will learn about the different jobs available in the tourism industry.
- You will be able to talk about jobs and their responsibilities.
- You will be able to introduce yourself and others, using correct grammar.

Vocabulary

- Flight Attendant
- Tour Guide
- Ground Crew
- Chauffeur
- Event Planner
- Card Dealer
- Maitre d'
- Interperter
- Exchange Bureau Officer
- Ticketing Agent
- Manager

- Bus Boy
- Immigration Officer
- House Keeper
- Cashier
- Chef
- Waiter/Waitress
- Tourist Information Officer
- Bellboy/Bellhop
- Travel Agent
- Bartender

Listening 1

Listen to the dialogues about jobs. Write the dialogue number next to the correct picture.

Key Phrases

What's your name?	My name is Sue.
What's his/her name?	His name is Allen./Her name is Sue
What are their names?	They're Jini and Tim.
Where are you from?	I'm from Korea.
Where is he/she from?	He's from Canada./She's from America.
Where are they from?	They're from the USA.
What do you do?	I'm a flight attendant.
What does he/she do?	He's a bellhop./She's a waitress.
What do they do?	They're bartenders.
Oh really, do you like it?	Yes, I do./No, I don't.
Does he/she like it?	Yes he does./No, she doesn't.
Do they like it?	Yes, they do./ No, they don't.
Where do you work?	I work for an airline.
Where does he/she work?	He works for a bar.
Where do they work?	They work for a tour company.
What are your responsibilities?	I serve customers.
What are his/her responsibilities?	He helps people./She serves customers.
What are their responsibilities?	They serve customers.
How long have you been working there?	For 6 months.
How long has he/she been working there?	For 1 year.
How long have they been working there?	For 2 weeks.

Please, Come Again

Activity

Write the answer using the clues.

1. What is her name? (Michelle)
2. What do you do? (tour guide)
3. What are his responsibilities? (introduces famous sites and guides city tours)
4. How long have they been working there? (3 years)
5. Do you like it? (yes)
6. What does she do? (flight attendant)
7. Does he like it? (no)
8. How long have you been working there? (4 months)
9. What are your responsibilities? (prepare food)
10. What do they do? (tourist information officers)

Activity

Read the responsibilities and write the job title.

Responsibility	She's a/an ......
• Interprets information into the customers' language	_____
• Prepares alcoholic drinks	_____
• Prepares food	_____
• Cleans rooms	_____
• Plans and organizes trips	_____
• Serves food	_____
• Introduces famous sights	_____
• Serves customers on an airplane	_____
• Hands out cards	_____
• Is a head waiter	_____
• Is a driver	_____
• Changes currency	_____

Listening 2

Listen to the dialogue, and write true or false. Correct the answers that are false.

1. Susan is a receptionist

	True	False
	T	F

....

2. Amy likes her job.

	True	False
	T	F

....

3. Amy has been working there for about 2 months.

	T	F

....

4. Amy answers the phone and takes reservations.

	T	F

....

5. Susan works for a coffee shop.

	T	F

....

6. Susan thinks her job is interesting.

	T	F

....

7. Susan would like to work for an airline.

	T	F

....

Please, Come Again

Listening 3

Listen to the dialogue, and complete the sentences. Then practice the conversation with your partner.

What do you do?

I'm a _____.

What are your _____?

I plan holidays and make _____.

How long have you been working there?

I've been working there for about _____.

_____ do you work?

I work in a travel agency called _____.

Oh really? I know that _____. Where are you from?

I'm from _____. What do you do?

I'm a _____.

Where do you work?

I work in a _____ called Coffee Breaks.

How long have you been working there?

I've been working there for about _____.

Speaking

In pairs, look at the chart. Student A and B can take turns asking and answering questions for the information to fill in their chart.

Student
A

Name?	Occupation?	Responsibilities?	Where?	How long?
Mary		serves passengers on an airplane	Airline	5 months
	Travel Agent		Travel Agency	
Tom		prepares food	Restaurant	
Chris				9 months
	Receptionist			8 years

Student B turn to page 9 ➡

011

Please, Come Again

Activity

Look at the information. With your partner write a short introduction about the jobs below and their responsibilities.

Then create an introduction for yourself in an imaginary job.

Include   Your name, where you are from, your job, your company name, your responsibilities, and how long you have worked there (make up a time).

Example :

Park Ji Sue
Adventure City Tours
Seoul, South Korea
Mobile: 010-789-1234
Office: 02-235-7894

Hello, my name is Park Ji Sue. I'm a tour guide. I work for Adventure City Tours in Seoul City. I take tourists to the famous places in Seoul and introduce my country. I have been working there for 2 years.

High Holiday Travel Agency
Tom Goody
Toronto, Canada
874-1256

Sleep Easy Hotels
Mary Macdonald
14 Green Street.
Went Town, California
864-1466

Michael James
London Limosine Express
- Airport service - Weddings
- City Tours   - Special events
Reservations call: 675-9876

Cherry Hill Casino
Tokyo, Japan
Wendy Baker, Card Dealer
02-1223-4455

Speaking

Student

B

Name?	Occupation?	Responsibilities?	Where?	How long?
	Flight Attendant			
Julie		plans and organizes trips		2 years
	Chef			1 year
	Waiter	serves food	Restaurant	
Amanda		gives information and takes reservations	Hotel	

Giving and
Asking Directions

Giving and
Asking Directions

Goals

- To be able to give and ask directions within a building.
- To be able to give and ask directions to someone on a street or on a subway.

Vocabulary

- Turn
- Right
- Behind
- Across from
- On the corner
- Between
- To the right of
- Intersection
- Rotary
- Around
- Go past
- 1 stop, 2 stops, etc

- Left
- In front of
- Next to
- In the corner
- At the corner
- To the left of
- 1 block, 2 blocks, etc
- Go straight
- Overpass / Underpass
- Bridge
- Transfer

Key Phrases

Excuse me, where is _____?

Excuse me, can you tell me where _____ is?

It's on the _second_ floor, next to the restrooms.

Go _two_ blocks, turn right at the bank and it is between the school and the supermarket.

Go _three more stops,_ transfer to the _blue line_ and go _two more stops_ to (subway station name).

Listening 1

Listen to the dialogues then number the name of the area and draw a line from the place to the correct floor. Some floors may be used twice.

____ Fitness center ●

____ Coffee shop ●

____ Exchange bureau ●

____ Parking lot ●

____ Restaurant ●

____ Payphones ●

Rooftop

5st floor

4st floor

3st floor

2st floor

1st floor

Basement

 Activity

In groups of two, take turns asking each other where different facilities are located within the hotel.

Example :

 Excuse me, where is the swimming pool?

 It's on the rooftop.

Dialogues :

 Excuse me, Can you tell me where the restaurant is?

 Sure, go straight for two blocks and turn right at the intersection. Keep going straight past the police station and it will be on your right. You can't miss it.

 Great, thank you.

 Excuse me, can you tell me where the photo shop is?

 Certainly, go straight for one block and turn right at the first intersection. Keep going straight to the next intersection and turn left. It will be on your right, across from the post office.

 Thank you so much.

Listening 2

school	bakery	police station	restaurant	department store
pharmacy	coffee shop	car center	post office	photo shop
bank	hair salon	grocery store	hotel	hospital

Start

Listen **to the directions and write the name of the place you arrive at on the map above.**

1. _____

2. _____

3. _____

4. _____

5. _____

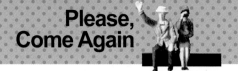

Activity

Look at the map from the last activity and write directions to the places listed below.

hotel	
police station	
school	
car center	

Practice asking questions about the location and giving directions.

Work in partners, each partner chooses a different location on the map. Partner A will then give that location to partner B who will write the directions to that location. Then practice dialogues similar to those in the examples.

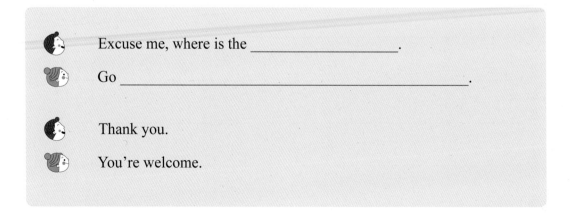

Excuse me, where is the _____.

Go _____.

Thank you.

You're welcome.

Let's Talk:

With a partner, choose one tourist attraction in your town that you would like
to introduce to someone who is visiting. Give directions from your school, or
the nearest subway station, to that tourist attraction.

Subways

Subway start point is
Dongjak station marked by
the indicator(📍).

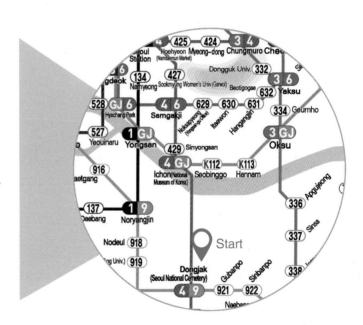

Dialogues :

Excuse me, can you tell me where Yaksu station is?

Sure, get on this line and go 3 stops north to Samgakji, transfer and
go 5 more stops on the Brown line. You will reach Yaksu in about 25
minutes.

Great, thank you for your help.

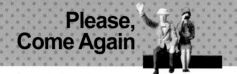

Practice

With a partner, choose a location on the map and make a short dialogue with directions on how to get there. Keep start point as Dongjak station.

After you finish with your dialogue, read the direction to the class and have the class try to guess where your final destination is.

What Time Does My Flight Leave?

What Time Does My Flight Leave?

Goals

- To be able to ask what time it is and to tell others the time.
- To give information about times of flights and other modes of transportation.

Vocabulary

- Hour
- After
- To
- A half past
- Late
- Delayed
- Every hour on the hour
- Midnight
- Ahead of schedule
- Every other day
- Hourly

- Minute
- Past
- A quarter after
- A quarter to
- On time
- Cancelled
- Once a week
- Noon
- Behind schedule
- Daily
- Postpone

Sentence Structures:

_____ past / after _____

(minutes)   (hour)

_____ to _____

(minutes)   (hour)

NOTE   Half past can only be used for 30 minutes. You can not say it is 30 after 6. You have to say it is half past 6.

Key Phrases

Excuse me, could you tell me what time it is? Yes, its ten past two. (2:10)

Can you tell me when the next train arrives? Sure, it arrives in 15 minutes.

Is the flight on time today? I'm sorry, The flight is delayed by 30 minutes.

How often do the buses run? They run every hour on the hour.

What time does your flight arrive? It is scheduled to arrive at a quarter to eight.

Listening 1

Listen to the *dialogues*. **Draw the times that you hear on the clocks and then write the times in words below.**

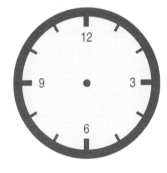
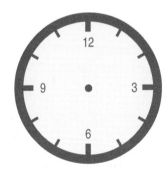
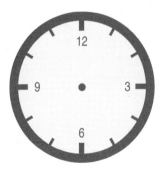

 Practice Activity

Make sentences using the pictures below. Practice using the sentences with a partner. Make sure the sentences are correct.

 bus   opens at

 subway   closes at

 bank   is served from

 lunch   leaves at

 supermarket arrives at

Sentence Structures:

 Excuse me, can you tell me what time the bank opens today?

 Yes sir, the bank opens at half past nine.

Activity

Look at the flight schedule and answer the questions in complete sentences.

✈ Flight Schedule

Departs	Arrives	Estimated Time of Departure	Estimated Time of Arrival
Incheon	Singapore	9:00	14:25
Busan	Kimpo	15:05	16:00
Daegu	Jeju	6:00	6:45
Incheon	Thailand	7:25	13:00
Kimpo	Busan	8:50	9:45

Excuse me, can you tell me what time the flight to Thailand leaves?

Yes sir, it leaves at _____.

Do you know what time the flight from Kimpo to Busan arrives?

Yes ma'am, it arrives at _____.

What time will we arrive in Singapore?

Our estimated time of arrival is _____.

What time does the flight depart for Kimpo?

Our estimated time of departure is _____.

When will we be arriving in Jeju?

We will be arriving at _____.

Restaurants:
Talking about Food and Preparation Methods

Restaurants:
Talking about Food and Preparation Methods

Goals

- You will learn about food commonly served in foreign hotel restaurants.
- You will be able to describe food to customers.
- You will be able to make recommendations to customers.
- You will learn about methods commonly used to prepare food and talk about them with customers.

Vocabulary

- Chocolate sauce
- Rare
- Imported beer
- Sorbert
- Well done
- Sour Grilled
- Steam
- Tart
- Fresh
- Stir-fry
- Filet Mignon
- Salty
- Deep fried
- Martini

- House wine
- Raspberry
- Medium
- Domestic beer
- Recommend
- Cream
- Spicy
- Saute
- Venison
- Juicy
- Bake
- Irish Coffee
- Marinade
- Roast

Practice

List popular food you know under the appropriate flavor.

Sweet	Sour	Spicy	Salty

Key Phrases

🔊	What do you recommend?	🔊	I recommend the *apple tart.* It's delicious.
🔊	What's the *lemon tart* like?	🔊	It's made with *fresh lemons*. It's *very sweet*.
🔊	How would you like it done?	🔊	I'd like it *medium rare.*
🔊	Do you have any *sour cream*?	🔊	Yes, we do./Sorry, we don't have any sour cream. But we do have some *salsa.*

Practice with a partner. Try to memorize the expressions.

Look at the cooking methods and food. Check all that apply.

Preparation method	Vegetables	Chicken	Beef	Fish	Rice
Saute					
Roast					
Stir-fry					
Steam					
Fry					
Bake					
Raw					
Grill					

Please, Come Again

Listening 1

Listen to the dialogues and complete the food orders.

Dialogue 1:

_____ _____ and a coffee.

Coffee with _____ .

Dialogue 2:

_____ steak

medium _____

Dialogue 3:

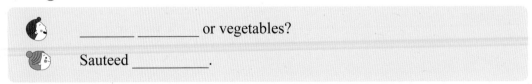

_____ _____ or vegetables?

Sauteed _____ .

Dialogue 4:

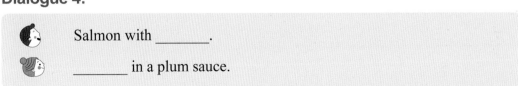

Salmon with _____ .

_____ in a plum sauce.

Dialogue

Fill in the blanks and practice the conversations with a partner.

Conversation 1:

What do you recommend?

I _____ the grilled steak. It's delicious.

Okay, I'd like to _____ the grilled steak.

And what's the chicken in plum sauce like?

I'd _____ it medium well done, please

Conversation 2:

Would you like a baked potato ____ vegetables?

I'd like vegetables please.

How would you like them done?

I'd _____ them steamed, please.

And for you sir?

I'd like sautéed vegetables, please.

Conversation 3:

What would _____ like for your entrée?

Hmm…. What's the salmon with almonds _____?

It's a grilled, fresh salmon. It's very flavorful.

And what's the chicken in plum sauce like?

It's roasted chicken. It's a _____ bit sweet.

Thank you. I'll try the salmon, please.

Please, Come Again

Activity 1

Answer the questions using the clues.

1. What do you recommend? (sorbert)
2. What's the grilled salmon like? (fresh salmon/juicy)
3. Do you have diet coke? (sorry/diet pepsi)
4. Would you like it with butter or without butter? (butter)
5. How would you like it done? (medium rare)
6. What's the raspberry tart like? (warm pastry/sweet)
7. Do you have any Cass beer? (sorry/Hite)
8. Would you like the vegetables steamed or sautéed? (steamed)
9. What do you recommend? (raw tuna with vegetables)
10. Do you have any cream? (yes)

Activity 2

Make a small menu for a Korean restaurant featuring popular Korean foods. Include in the menu: appetizers, entrees, desserts, and drinks.

With a partner, practice recommending and talking about dishes on the menu.

Important

Desserts are not drinks, they are food such as cake, ice cream or other sweet treats.

Example :

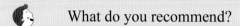 What do you recommend?

 I recommend the Bibimbap. It's delicious.

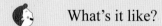 What's it like?

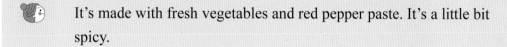 It's made with fresh vegetables and red pepper paste. It's a little bit spicy.

Restaurants:
Can I Take Your Order?

Restaurants:
Can I Take Your Order?

Goals

- You will be able to politely take a customer's order in a restaurant.
- You will be able to ask and answer questions about the customer's order.

Please, Come Again

- Appetizer/Starter
- Main Course
- Dessert
- Order
- Refill
- Side Dish
- Beverage
- Vegetarian
- Soup of the day
- Domestic

- Entrée
- Side Order/Side Dish
- Dressing
- Care for
- Brunch
- Specials
- Set Menu
- Menu
- Imported

Key Phrases

Do you have a reservation?	Yes. The name is ………/No. I don't.
Are you ready to order?	Yes, I am./Can you give us a few minutes?
What would you like to start with?	I'd like the soup of the day.
What would you like to order?	I'd like the grilled chicken.
What (side dish) would you like with that?	I'll have a green salad.
Would you like something to drink?	I'll have a glass of red wine, please.
Would you like some dessert or coffee?	Yes, I'll have the cheese cake./No, thank you.
Is that everything?/ Would you like anything else?	That's everything. Thanks.
That comes to 60,000 Won.	Here you are.

Practice with a partner. Try to memorize the expressions.

Practice

Write the question to match the answer.

1. _____?

   Yes, the name is Park.

2. _____?

   Yes please, I'll have the filet mignon.

3. _____?

   I'd like it medium rare, please.

4. _____?

   I'd like the stir-fried vegetables.

5. _____?

   Yes, I'll have a mineral water, please.

6. _____?

   Yes, I'll have the cheese cake, please.

7. _____?

   That's everything.

 Listening 1

Listen to the conversation. Decide if these sentences are true or false. Correct the sentences that are false.

1. The waiter asks the customer if he has a reservation.

_____

2. Today's special is grilled salmon.

_____

3. The customer would not like a drink.

_____

4. The customer would like cheese and bread as an appetizer.

_____

5. The customer would like the grilled salmon.

_____

6. The side dishes are salad, baked potato, and rice.

_____

7. The customer would like a side of rice.

_____

Dialogue

Practice the dialogue in pairs. You can substitute the underlined items with your own choice of food.

Here's your menu.

Thank you.

Would you care for a drink?

Yes, please. I'll have a *martini*.

Are you ready to order now?

Yes, I am.

What would you like to start with?

I'd like the *fried potato plate*.

What would you like for the main course?

I'd like the *trout with almonds*.

And what would you like with that?

I'd like the *mixed vegetables*, please.

Okay, so that's a *fried potato plate* to start, and the *trout with almonds with a side of vegetables* for the main course. Would you like anything else?

That's everything, thank you.

Enjoy your meal.

Please, Come Again

Activity

With a partner use the menu and the order form to take turns being the server and the guest.

Guest — Look at the menu and decide what you would like to eat and drink.

Server — Take the guests' order.

■ Look at the dialogue on page 43 and use key phrases if you need help.

The Seoul Style Restaurant

Appetizers	Price
Soup of the day	5,000 Won
Cheese and bread	9,000 Won
Garden salad	6,000 Won
Fresh fruit	6,000 Won

Entrees
All entrees are available with your choice of salad, fries, or mixed vegetables

Charbroiled steak	20,000 Won
Chicken in nut sauce	18,000 Won
Roast beef sandwich with mushroom gravy	15,000 Won
Baked salmon	25,000 Won
Vegetable stir fry	12,000 Won

Beverages

Mineral water	3,000 Won
Soft drinks – cola, cider, orange, grape	2,500 Won
Imported beers	6,000 Won
Domestic beers	4,000 Won

Dessert

Ice cream- vanilla, chocolate, strawberry	4,000 Won
Chocolate cake	5,000 Won
Strawberry cheese cake	5,000 Won
Banana pudding	3,000 Won

The Seoul Style Restaurant

Quantity	Items Ordered	Price
_____	_____	_____
_____	_____	_____
_____	_____	_____
_____	_____	_____
_____	_____	_____
_____	_____	_____
	Total:	_____

Thank you, please come again.

Travel Agencies:

Where Would You Like to Travel?

Travel Agencies:
Where Would You Like to Travel?

Goals

- To be able to give information about travel packages.
- To answer customers questions about traveling.

Please, Come Again

Vocabulary

- Package tour
- Attractions
- Via
- Cancellation Fee
- Promotion
- Half/Full day
- Availability
- Arrive(al)
- Travel Insurance

- Itinerary
- Connecting flight
- Transfer
- Sightseeing
- Leisure
- Duration
- Brochure
- Depart(ure)

Key Phrases

Travel Agent:

How can I help you?

Where would you like to go?

When would you like to go?

When would you like to return?

Would you like first class or economy, sir?

I'm sorry we have nothing available for that date.

Would you like a package tour?

Would you like me to send you a brochure?

Would you like me to make a reservation for you?

That will come to _____ plus tax.

Customer:

I'd like to book a ticket please.

I'd like to go to (place).

I'd like to leave on (date).

I'd like to return on (date).

Do you have any promotions?

Are there any package tours?

How much is the total?

Dialogues :

1

Travel agent — Good afternoon, how may I help you?

Customer — Yes, I would like to book a ticket to Germany, please.

Travel agent — Certainly sir, when would you like to leave?

Customer — I'd like to leave on August 7th.

Travel agent — And when would you like to return?

Customer — I would like to return on August 14th.

Travel agent — Would you like first class or economy, sir?

Customer — Economy, please.

Travel agent — Okay, let me check for you... thank you for waiting sir, there is one seat left in economy for those dates.

Customer — Thank you and how much is the total?

Travel agent — That will come to $976 plus tax.

Customer — Sounds great, thank you. I'll take it.

2

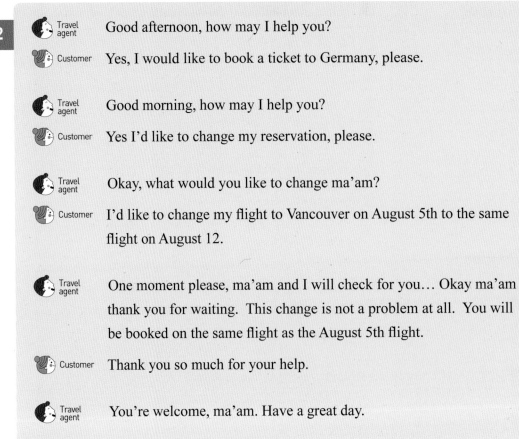

Travel agent: Good afternoon, how may I help you?

Customer: Yes, I would like to book a ticket to Germany, please.

Travel agent: Good morning, how may I help you?

Customer: Yes I'd like to change my reservation, please.

Travel agent: Okay, what would you like to change ma'am?

Customer: I'd like to change my flight to Vancouver on August 5th to the same flight on August 12.

Travel agent: One moment please, ma'am and I will check for you... Okay ma'am thank you for waiting. This change is not a problem at all. You will be booked on the same flight as the August 5th flight.

Customer: Thank you so much for your help.

Travel agent: You're welcome, ma'am. Have a great day.

Activity

Match the travel agents question to the appropriate answer. Put the number of the answer in the blanks below.

Where would you like to travel? _____

When would you like to leave? _____

When would you like to return? _____

Would you like first class or economy? _____

How would you like to pay? _____

① I would like first class, please.

② I'd like to return on June 24th.

③ I would like to go to Spain.

④ I'd like to pay by Visa.

⑤ I'd like to leave on June 12th.

Please, Come Again

Listening 1

Listen to the dialogue and fill in the blanks below.

Travel agent _____, how may I help you?

Customer I'd like to make a _____, please.

Travel agent Okay, where would you _____, sir?

Customer I'd like to go to _____.

Travel agent Great, and when would you like to leave?

Customer I'd like to leave on _____.

Travel agent And when would you like to return?

Customer I'd like to return on _____.

Travel agent Would you like to fly first class or economy, sir?

Customer _____, please.

Travel agent One moment please, let me _____ for you...
Thank you for waiting. I am very sorry sir, but we
_____ first class seats available but there
is one economy seat open.

Customer Okay, that's fine, _____.

Travel agent May I have your name please, sir?

Customer _____ Mr. John Smith.

Travel agent May I have your _____, Mr. Smith?

Customer Yes it's ML024132.

Travel agent Sir, the total comes to $745 _____.

Customer Okay, I'll pay by credit card.

More Practice

Using the information in the chart create a dialogue with a partner. One of you will be a travel agent and the other will be a customer. Make reservations for each customer.

Name	Passport number	Destination	departure date	return date	cost
Ms. Kim Smith	ML0251789	England	03-Jan	21-Jan	$1,325
Mr. Steven Jones	JX2527846	Mexico	11-Nov	17-Nov	$976
Mrs. Jane Dell	KH636848	Cambodia	04-Jul	14-Jul	$650
Mr. Robert Harvey	DN257368	Thailand	21-Mar	31-Mar	$720

Review :

Unscramble the words to make proper sentences or questions

1.   return When like you would to

           _____?

2.   available sorry we I'm nothing date for have that

           _____?

3.   promotions have Do any you

           _____?

4.   economy Would first like class you or

           _____?

5.   package Would tour like you a

           _____?

Hotel Facilities and Services:
Do You Have a Swimming Pool?

Hotel Facilities and Services:
Do You Have a Swimming Pool?

Goals

- To be able to give information about hotel facilities.
- To be able to tell guests about services that are provided at the hotel.

Vocabulary

- Fitness center
- Swimming pool
- Vending machines
- Taxi/limo service
- Laundry services
- Complimentary
- Restaurant
- Room service
- Room types
  standard / double / twin / suite
- Rate (cost)
- Exchange bureau
- Seating capacity

- Gift shop
- Sauna
- Travel office (agency)
- Handicapped facilities
- Wake-up call
- Coffee shop
- Bar
- Underground parking
- Information desk
- Conference room
- Available
- Internet access

Key Phrases

Is there a parking lot available?

Where is the _____ ?

Where are the _____ ?

Is there a/an _____ in this hotel?

Are there any _____ in this hotel?

What time does the _____ open?

Would you like a wake-up call?

How much is the rate for a standard room?

Dialogue

1

Guest   Is there a swimming pool in this hotel?

Receptionist   Yes, there is. It is on the 4th floor.

Guest   What time does it open in the morning?

Receptionist   It opens at 6 a.m., every morning.

Guest   Great, can I get an extra towel for the pool?

Receptionist   Sir, towels are provided on the pool deck for our guests.

Guest   Oh great, thank you very much.

Receptionist   You're welcome sir, have a nice day.

Guest   You too.

2

Receptionist   Good afternoon ma'am, how may I help you?

Guest   I was wondering if you can book a city tour for me here for tomorrow?

Receptionist   Certainly, the city tour leaves at 9 a.m., everyday.

Guest   Great!

Receptionist   Okay, may I have your name please, ma'am.

Guest   Yes, it's Ms. Smith.

Receptionist   And your first name?

Guest   It's Jane.

Receptionist	Alright Ms. Smith, one seat on the city tour tomorrow. Is that correct?
Guest	Yes, that's correct, thank you.
Receptionist	You're welcome, is there anything else I can do for you today?
Guest	Actually, yes. Can I get a wake-up call for 7 a.m. tomorrow?
Receptionist	No problem at all, Ms Smith, a wake-up call for 7 a.m. tomorrow.
Guest	Yes, thank you.
Receptionist	Thank you and have a nice day.

Listening 1

Listen and fill in the blanks.

1. The restaurant opens for lunch _____ 11:00 _____ 2:30.

2. What _____ _____ the exchange bureau open?

3. Can I get a _____ for 7:00 a.m.

4. _____ is the coffee shop.

5. Do all the rooms _____ internet access?

6. Our conference room has _____ for 200 people.

7. Please enjoy our _____ continental breakfast in the morning.

8. Where can I _____ a city tour?

9. Can you please _____ me a taxi?

10. How late is room service _____?

Activity

Draw a line to match the image to the service or facility.

- Currency exchange bureau

- Coffee shop

- Swimming pool

- Cocktail bar

- Payphones

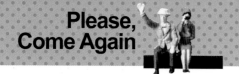
Grammar Focus:

When asking questions about the services available in a hotel you can say

"Is there a _____" or "Are there any _____."

"Is there a/an _____ in the hotel?" would be used for a singular noun (one thing).

"Are there any _____ in the hotel?" would be used for plural nouns (more than one).

◄ To answer these questions you can say :

Yes, there is. / No, there isn't.
Or

Yes there are. / No, there aren't.

◄ Example:

Is there an exchange bureau in the hotel?

Yes, there is.

Or

Are there any public restrooms in the hotel?

No, there aren't.

Grammar Practice:

Make sentences and answers using the grammar focus information.

1. payphones / (Yes)

2. swimming pool / (No)

3. internet access / (Yes)

4. gift shop / (Yes)

5. vending machines / (No)

6. fitness center / (No)

7. travel agency / (Yes)

8. restaurant / (Yes)

9. parking spaces / (No)

10. coffee shop / (Yes)

Hotel Reservations:
For How Many Nights?

Hotel Reservations:
For How Many Nights?

Goals

- To be able to make reservations in a hotel.
- To answer questions about hotel accommodations and prices.
- To learn basic grammar; There is / There are and Is there…? / Are there…?

Please, Come Again

- Address
- Confirm
- Guest
- Twin room
- Suite
- Reservation
- Travelers check(cheque)

- Arrival date
- Credit card
- Method of Payment
- Double room
- Reservation Number
- Room type
- Expiration date

Key Phrases

May I have your name please?	
Could you spell that please?	
When will you be arriving?	I'll be arriving on June 6th.
What kind of room would you like?	I'd like a double room, please.
Would you like smoking or non-smoking?	Non-smoking please.
For how many nights?	3 nights
Will you be traveling alone?	
How will you be paying?	I'll pay by credit card. Do you accept Visa?
May I have the card number please?	Yes, it's 1234-5678-9102.
May I have the expiry date please?	Yes, it's 05/25 (May 2025).
I can confirm your reservation.	
I'm sorry we're fully booked	

Dialogue

1

Receptionist Good afternoon. This is the Rainforest Hotel. How may I help you?

Customer I'd like to make a reservation please.

Receptionist Okay ma'am, when will you be arriving?

Customer On May 5th.

Receptionist Alright, one moment please and I will check availability.

Customer Thanks.

Receptionist I'm very sorry ma'am. We are fully booked on May 5th.

Customer Oh, that's too bad. Thank you.

2

Receptionist Good morning. This is the Southside Hotel. How may I help you?

Customer Hi, I'd like to make a reservation please.

Receptionist Certainly sir, may I have your name please?

Customer Yes, its Edward Hintz.

Receptionist Okay, could you spell that out please, sir?

Customer Yes, its H-I-N-T-Z.

Receptionist Thank you, Mr. Hintz. And when will you be arriving?

Customer On February 18th.

Receptionist And for how many nights?

Customer For 2 nights, please.

Receptionist Okay, and what kind of room would you like Mr. Hintz?

Customer A double room, please.

Receptionist Would you like smoking or non-smoking?

Customer Non-smoking, please.

Receptionist Certainly, and how will you be paying sir?

Customer By credit card, please. Do you take MasterCard?

Receptionist Yes sir. May I have the card number please?

Customer Sure, its 1234-5230-6475-1231.

Receptionist Thank you and may I have the expiry date as well?

Customer Sure, it's 07/25 (July 2025).

Receptionist Alright, thank you Mr. Hintz. I can confirm your reservation. That's a double room for 2 nights from February 18th. Is this correct?

Customer Yes, great.

Receptionist Okay. We look forward to seeing you on February 18th. Have a great day sir.

Listening 1

Listen to the *dialogue* and fill in the reservation form.

Cannon Inn

Name: _____
                   Last   First

Address: _____

_____

Telephone: _____

Arrival date _____

Departure date: _____

Room type: ____ Double $75.00

             ____ Twin $110.00

             ____ Suite $189.00

____ Smoking   _____ Non-smoking

Method of Payment: ____ Cash

                  ____ Credit card   Card name:_____

Card number: _____   Expiration date: _____

Confirming reservations:

Dialogue

Guest information:

Name: John Smith	
Room type: Double room	
Arrival: October 9th	
Number of nights: 4 nights	

Okay, sir. I can confirm your reservation. You have a double room from October 9th for 4 nights. Is that correct?

Activity

Practice confirming reservations with the information below then practice pronunciation with a partner.

❶ Guest information:

Name: Michael Emmitt	
Room type: Double room	
Arrival: April 23rd	
Number of nights: 3 nights	

❷ **Guest information:**

Name: Jim MacDonald	
Room type: Suite	
Arrival: September 14th	
Number of nights: 6 nights	

❸ **Guest information:**

Name: Jane Mcrae	
Room type: Twin room	
Arrival: March 11th	
Number of nights: 2 nights	

Unit Review:

Create a dialogue and fill out the registration form about your partner.

Inspire Hotel

Name: _____
                                     Last   First

Address: _____

_____

Telephone: _____

Arrival date _____

Departure date: _____

Room type: _____ Double $75.00

              _____ Twin $110.00

              _____ Suite $189.00

_____ Smoking   _____ Non-smoking

Method of Payment: _____ Cash

                             _____ Credit card   Card name:_____

Card number: _____   Expiration date: _____

Enjoy Your Stay!

Enjoy Your Stay!

Goals

- To learn basic communication skills for working at a hotel front desk.
- To be able to ask and answer appropriate questions for checking guests in and out.

Please, Come Again

Vocabulary

- Register
- Passport number
- Emergency contact
- Signature/sign
- Key card
- Nationality
- Arrive
- Double room
- Suite

- Registration card
- Front desk
- Next destination
- Fill in/fill out
- Walk-in
- Swipe/imprint
- Depart
- Twin room

Key Phrases

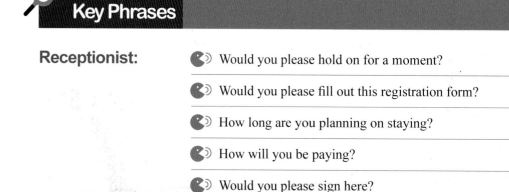

Receptionist:

Would you please hold on for a moment?

Would you please fill out this registration form?

How long are you planning on staying?

How will you be paying?

Would you please sign here?

Your room is on the _____ st/nd/rd/th floor

Here is your receipt and keycard.

The bellhop can show you to your room.

I hope you have a pleasant stay.

It comes to a total of _____ Won.

Here is your change.

Customer:

Are there any rooms available for tonight?

I have a reservation for tonight.

What are the room rates?

Which floor is it on?

I'd like to check out today.

Can I have the bill for my room, please?

What is the check-out time?

Can you hold my luggage until 4 pm?

Check-in Dialogues:

1

Receptionist   Good morning, can I help you?

Customer   Yes, my name is Mr. John Smith and I have a room reserved for tonight.

Receptionist   Okay sir, let me check for you... That's a double room for 2 nights?

Customer   Yes.

Receptionist   Would you please fill out this registration form, Mr. Smith?

Customer   Certainly.

Receptionist   And can you sign here, please?

Customer   Sure.

Receptionist   Thank you, sir. Here is your receipt and key card. The bellhop can show you to your room.

Customer   Thank you.

Receptionist   Thank you very much and I hope you have a pleasant stay.

2

Receptionist	Good afternoon ma'am. Can I help you?
Customer	Yes, do you have any rooms available for tonight?
Receptionist	Yes we do. What kind of room would you like ma'am?
Customer	Just a double room, please.
Receptionist	And how long are you planning on staying?
Customer	For 2 nights. What is the room rate?
Receptionist	Its 40,000 Won per night.
Customer	That's okay.
Receptionist	Would you please fill out this registration form?
Customer	Sure.
Receptionist	How would you like to pay?
Customer	Do you take credit cards?
Receptionist	Yes, may I have your card, please?
Customer	Here you are.
Receptionist	Thank you. And can you sign here, please?
Customer	Okay.
Receptionist	Here is your receipt and room key. Your room is on the 8th floor. I hope you have a pleasant stay.
Customer	Thank you.

Activity

Using the information in the boxes below, create a dialogue between a receptionist and a customer.

Name	Mr Andrew Barnes
Room	Double, 4 nights
Passport number	JX052394
Address	241 James Avenue, Washington DC, 44214

Name	Ms. Jane Munroe
Room	Double, 2 nights
Passport number	ML124624
Address	12 Market Street, Toronto, Ontario, H4J-2G7

Name	Mr. Charles Kincade
Room	Twin, 3 nights
Passport number	HG425758
Address	Apartment 202, Sunny Towers, Vancouver, BC, M4D-5F3

Name	Mr. and Mrs. William Molson
Room	Honeymoon Suite, 3 nights
Passport number	KL523683
Address	41 Aroma Apartments, 466 Quing Xi street, Bejing, China, 499124

Listening 1

Listen to the *dialogue* and fill in the blanks.

Receptionist   Good evening sir, may I help you?

Customer   Yes, my name is Jim MacDonald. I have a room _____ for tonight.

Receptionist   Okay, let me check Mr. MacDonald... That's a _____?

Customer   Yes it is.

Receptionist   Okay, can you _____ registration form please?

Customer   Sure, here you are.

Receptionist   Thank you, sir. Here is your _____. Your room is on the _____.

Customer   Thank you.

Receptionist   Thank you. And I hope you enjoy your stay.

Check-in Dialogues:

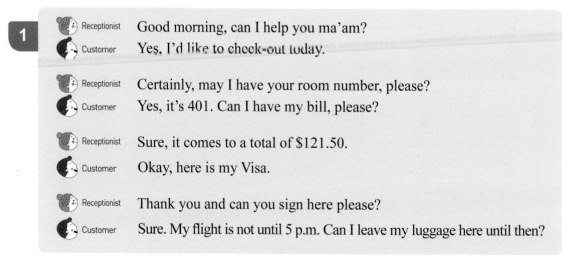

1

Receptionist   Good morning, can I help you ma'am?

Customer   Yes, I'd like to check-out today.

Receptionist   Certainly, may I have your room number, please?

Customer   Yes, it's 401. Can I have my bill, please?

Receptionist   Sure, it comes to a total of $121.50.

Customer   Okay, here is my Visa.

Receptionist   Thank you and can you sign here please?

Customer   Sure. My flight is not until 5 p.m. Can I leave my luggage here until then?

	Receptionist	Certainly. If you bring it to the desk, we will look after it for you.
	Customer	Great, thanks a lot.
	Receptionist	No problem, ma'am.

Listening 2

Listen to the *dialogue* and fill in the blanks.

Check-in Dialogues:

1

	Receptionist	Good morning, sir. _____?
	Customer	Yes, I would like to _____ today. What's the usual check out time?
	Receptionist	It is 11 a.m.
	Customer	Okay, _____?
	Receptionist	Sure, may I _____?
	Customer	Yes, it's _____.
	Receptionist	Okay, let me check that for you, sir. The total comes to _____. _____.
	Customer	I'll pay _____. Here you are.
	Receptionist	Thank you, and _____?
	Customer	_____.
	Receptionist	Okay, thank you sir. _____ and I hope _____.
	Customer	Thank you.

Please, Come Again

Activity

Look at the bill below and answer the questions.

Billing Mr. Robert Martin Room: 0601

Department	Date	Amount	Quantity	Total
Accommodation	2019-07-21	55,000 Won	2	110,000 Won
Room service	2019-07-21	16,000 Won	1	16,000 Won
Mini bar	2019-07-21	9,000 Won	1	9,000 Won
Telephone	2019-07-21	7,000 Won	1	7,000 Won
			Total	142,000 Won

1. What room did Mr. Martin stay in?

   _____

2. How many nights did Mr. Martin stay?

   _____

3. How much did Mr. Martin spend on room service?

   _____

4. What was the total for Mr. Martin's bill?

   _____

Listen and Practice (Listening 2의 Dialogue 활용)

Put the following sentences in the correct order to make up a dialogue about checking out. Check your answer by listening to the correct *dialogue*.

_____ Thank you and can you sign here, please?

_____ It is 11 a.m.

_____ Thank you.

_____ Sure, may I have your room number, please?

_____ Certainly.

_____ Good morning, sir. Can I help you?

_____ Okay, let me check that for you, sir. The total comes to $142.50. How would you like to pay?

_____ Yes, I would like to check-out later today. What is the check-out time?

_____ I'll pay by Visa, please. Here you are.

_____ Yes it's 1112.

_____ Okay. Thank you sir, here is your receipt, and I hope you enjoyed your stay with us.

_____ Okay, can I pay my bill now?

◼ Now work with a partner and practice the completed dialogue

Tour guides:

What Sights Will I See on the Tour?

Tour guides:
What Sights Will I See on the Tour?

Goals

- You will be able to answer questions about cost, duration and schedules.
- You will be able to talk about what sights the customer will see on the tour.
- You will be able to describe itineraries and answer questions about tour.

Vocabulary

- Tour
- Attractions
- Explore
- Package deal
- City Tour
- Pick up
- Ancient
- Palace
- Temple

- Sightseeing/the sights
- Duration
- Brochure
- Include
- Itinerary
- Drop off
- Tombs
- Ruins
- Gallery

Practice

Make a list of all the famous sights in Korea including Palaces, Tombs, Galleries, Ruins, and Nature.

Key Phrases

I would like to get information about city bus tours.	There are many tours to show you the sights.
I would like to book a city bus tour.	Sure, no problem.
How much will the tour cost?	It costs *45,000* won.
What sites will I visit on the tour?	You'll visit the *old city ruins and some temples*.
What will we visit first?	In the morning we'll visit the *Kings Tomb*.
What's included in the cost?	The tour includes *lunch*, and *transportation*.
When will the tour leave?	The bus leaves from the *tourist information office* at 7 a.m.
When will the tour return?	The bus returns at *8 p.m.*

Activity

Write the vocabulary word to match the definition below.

1. Visiting and seeing places and objects of interest

2. A grave or other place of burial.

3. The products or services all included for one set price.

4. A detailed plan for a journey. A list of places to visit, plan of travel.

5. Traveling around from place to place.

6. The remains of a building, city, etc.

A. Ruins	B. Sightseeing
C. Itinerary	D. Tomb
E. Tour	F. Package deal

Please, Come Again

Listening 1

Listen and put the conversation in the correct order. Then practice with your partner.

Conversation

Tourist	I'd like to get some information about day tours of the city.
Guide	The tour includes a restaurant, breakfast, and transportation. Lunch is not included.

Guide	Okay, that will be 60 dollars each, please. Have a great trip!
Guide	The tour bus will leave from your hotel at 9:30 a.m.

Guide	The tour will return at 6 p.m.
Tourist	What sites will I see?

Guide	Korea-Seoul Tours, how can I help you?
Guide	Sure, no problem.

Tourist	What is included in the cost?
Guide	You'll see the National Gallery, City Park, and an ancient temple.

Tourist	When will the tour leave?
Tourist	I would like to book a city bus tour for tomorrow.

Tourist	Okay, I'll book two seats, please.
Guide	Sure, no problem. There are many tours you can take to show you the sights.

Tourist	And when will the tour return?

086

Activity

Look at the itinerary. Ask and answer questions about the tour with your partner.

Example Questions

 What sites will I visit on the tour?

 How much will the tour cost?

 What's included in the cost?

 When will the tour leave?

 When will the tour return?

Discovery Beijing
One Day Tours

All Tours are 50 dollars U.S and include Breakfast, Dinner and Transportation.
Tours start everyday at 7 a.m.

7 a.m.	Pick up at City Tours Main Office.
Morning	Watch the national flag rising and tour around Tian'anmen Square. Have Breakfast in a Traditional Chinese Restaurant. (breakfast included in the cost)
10 a.m.	Walk around Imperial Palace. Take picture of ancient Chinese palace.
Afternoon	Have lunch at street vendor (lunch not included).
1 p.m.	Take a tour of the Temple of Heaven. Have some traditional Chinese tea and watch daily street performances.
Evening	Have a boat tour and watch the sunset at Beijing Summer Palace. Have dinner at Chinese Duck Restaurant.
8 p.m.	Drop off at City Tours Main Office.

Activity

Step One

Plan an itinerary for a 1 day trip anywhere in Korea. Include hotels, travel time, meals and sightseeing.

Example:

Day one	New York, USA
7:30 a.m.	Get up. Have breakfast in the hotel.
9:30 a.m.	Arrive at the Museum of Natural History for a guided tour.
12:30 p.m.	Take the bus to Central Park. Have a picnic lunch.
2:30 p.m.	Take the bus to the Empire State Building.

Step Two

Using your sample itinerary, write a short conversation between a tour guide and a tourist who is interested in taking the tour.

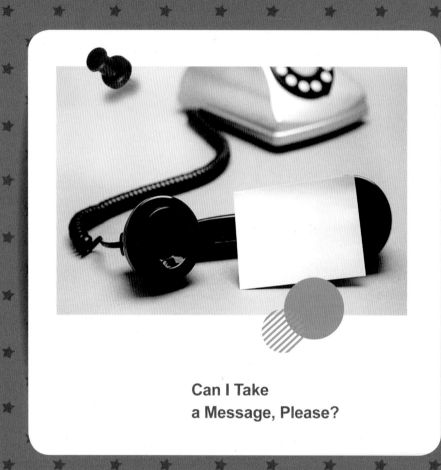

**Can I Take
a Message, Please?**

Can I Take a Message, Please?

Goals

- You will be able to answer the telephone politely.
- You will be able to explain when someone's not available and take a phone message.
- You will be able to fill in phone message cards accurately.

Vocabulary

- Busy
- Cell phone
- Leave a message
- Received
- Wrong number
- Confirmation
- Hold the line
- Extension
- Call back
- Long Distance
- Local call
- Unavailable
- Speaking
- Urgent

- Request
- One moment
- Cancel
- Important
- Will call again
- Please call
- Meeting
- Memo
- Appointment
- A.S.A.P.(As Soon As Possible)
- Transfer
- Step out
- Connect

Key Phrases

How can I help you?　　　　　　　　　Yes, I would like to speak to *the manager* please.

May I ask who's calling?　　　　　　　This is *Miss. Lee.*

One moment please, I'll put you through.　　Thank you.

He's busy/unavailable/in a meeting right now.　Yes, please have him call me back

Would you like to leave a message?　　　(as soon as possible).

Where can you be reached at?　　　　　I can be reached at 010-8987-1234.

When is the best time for him to return your call?　Have him call me before 6 p.m.

Practice

Look at the memo and answer the questions.

Easy Sleep Hotel and Apartments
Memo

To: Mr. Jon Kelly   *Date*: 12/01

From: Ms. Jessica Wilson   *Time*: 8:30 p.m.

Office: Korean tours   *Phone*: 010-4154-9871

_____ Will call again   _____ Please call

_____ Returned your call   _____ Urgent

MESSAGE:

Wants an e-mail confirmation of her reservation from Nov. 12th to 15th.

Please e-mail: j.wilson@koreantours.com

Message taken By: Lily MacDonald

---

1. Who did Ms. Wilson leave the message with?

2. What is the date?

3. Who was the message for?

4. Where does Ms. Wilson work?

5. Why was Ms. Wilson calling?

6. Who took the message?

Please, Come Again

Listening 1

Listen to the *dialogue* and check what you hear.

1. Mr Jonson	Unavailable	___	In a meeting	___	Busy	___
2. Manager	Will call again	___	Returned your call	___	Please call	___
3. Miss Lee	Wants to cancel	___	Wants to change the date	___	Wrong number	___
4. Manager	Urgent	___	Telephoned	___	Will call again	___

Activity

Write a sentence using the vocabulary words

Wrong number_____

Transfer_____

Local Call_____

Appointment_____

Cancel_____

Leave a message_____

Unavailable_____

Urgent_____

Hold_____

A.S.A.P_____

Listening 2

Listen to the conversation and fill-in the message pad where possible. Then practice the conversations with your partner.

Dialogue 1

A-List Hotel
Memo

To: _____   *Date*: _____

From: _____

OFFICE: _____   *PH*: _____

_____ *Telephoned*   _____ *Please call*

_____ *Will call again*   _____ *Important*

MESSAGE: _____

_____

_____

Message taken By: _____

Dialogue 2

Seoul City Tours
SOMEONE CALLED

To: _____   *Date*: _____

From: _____

Message

OFFICE: _____   *PH*: _____

OF: _____

_____ *Telephoned*   _____ *Please call*

_____ *Will call again*   _____ *Important*

MESSAGE: _____

_____

_____

Message taken By: _____

096

Activity

Step One

In pairs write a conversation between a receptionist and a caller. Be sure to include:

1. The company name
2. Who is calling
3. Who the message is for
4. Return phone number
5. What is the message and action to be taken
6. Who took the message

Step Two

Take turns reading your conversation to other groups. Have them fill-in the memo card.

Memo

_____

To: _____   *Date*: _____

From: _____   *Time*: _____

Of: _____   *Phone*: _____

_____ *Will call again*   _____ *Please call*

_____ *Returned your call*   _____ *Telephoned*

MESSAGE:

_____

_____

Message taken By: _____

Flight Attendants:
Ground Crew

Flight Attendants:
Ground Crew

Goals

- You will be able to check-in a customer for their flight.
- You will be able to ask and answer questions about a customer's boarding pass.
- You will learn the key words used at an airport check-in counter and while boarding.

Vocabulary

- Aisle Seat
- Seat assignment
- Economy class
- Excess weight
- Baggage tag
- Carry-on items
- Boarding
- On time
- Passport
- Flight number
- Prohibited
- Check-in
- Boarding
- Departure

- Window Seat
- First class
- Baggage claim
- Scale
- Suitcase
- Gate
- Delay
- Cancelled
- Boarding pass
- Announcement
- Security
- Departure lounge
- Get an upgrade

Key Phrases

Where are you travelling to? — I'm going to _Vancouver._

May I see your ticket and passport, please? — Here you are.

How many bags do you have to check in? — _2_ suitcases.

Could you please place your bags on the scale? — Sure.

Do you have any carry-on bags? — Yes, I have 1 piece. A _laptop bag._

What time is boarding? — Your boarding time is _1:20._

What is the gate number? — You're boarding from gate _25D_.

Would you like a window or aisle seat? — I'd like a _window_ seat, please.

I'd like an _aisle_ seat, please.

Practice

Look at the boarding pass and answer the questions.

WORLD GLOBAL AIRLINES	WGA
Class ECONOMY CLASS Flight & date WG 1191 / 29/12/2019 Gate A12 Seat 24C Boarding time > 0600- FLIGHT DEPARTS @ 0630 Departing from SAN FRANCISCO (SFO) Destination TORONTO (YYZ) Passenger Name MONTOYA/ALLEN P. BOARDING PASS 1575-247-2446-3567-3556-T3943	Seat & Class 24C ECON Destination TOR Remarks Vegetarian Meal

What is the passenger's name?

What airline is the passenger flying with?

What is the flight number?

What class is the passenger flying on?

What is the gate number?

What is the seat number?

Where is the passenger departing from?

What is the destination?

What is the boarding time?

Activity

Write ten sentences using the vocabulary words below.

Baggage tag	Suitcase	Boarding	Check-in
On time	Gate	Prohibited	Get an upgrade
Departure	Passport	Departure lounge	

1. _____

2. _____

3. _____

4. _____

5. _____

6. _____

7. _____

8. _____

9. _____

10. _____

Listening 1

Listen to the *dialogue* and answer the questions in full sentences.

Where would the passenger like to sit?

_____

How many bags will the passenger check-in?

_____

What is the boarding time?

_____

What is the gate number?

_____

When should the customer go through security check?

_____

How much does the passenger's suitcase weigh?

_____

Please, Come Again

Listening 1

Practice the dialogue with your partner

Dialogue

Check-in-Clerk	Good morning. May I see your ticket and passport, please?
Passenger	Sure, here you are.
Check-in-Clerk	I see you are going to Hawaii.
Passenger	Yes, that's right.
Check-in-Clerk	How many bags do you have to check-in?
Passenger	One bag and a set of golf clubs.
Check-in-Clerk	Do you have any carry-on bags?
Passenger	Yes, I have one.
Check-in-Clerk	Great. Your boarding time is 10:45 a.m. Please go through security check 30 minutes before boarding.
Passenger	And what is the gate number?
Check-in-Clerk	It's 15B.
Passenger	Thanks.
Check-in-Clerk	Okay, enjoy your flight!

Activity

Look at the passenger information, ask and answer questions about flight check-in information with your partner.

Passenger's Name	Destination	Number of Suitcases	Number of Carry-ons	Boarding time	Gate Number
Mrs. Mary Jonson	London	2	1	3:25 p.m.	12C
Mr. Ed Thompson	Bangkok	0	2	12:45 a.m.	5
Dr. Linda Davis	Siem Reap	1	2	9:00 a.m.	21
Miss. Sue Howardson	Chicago	3	0	7:20 a.m.	18B

Currencies and Transactions

Currencies and Transactions

- To be able to ask and answer questions about prices of items.
- To learn about different currencies in different areas of the world.

Please, Come Again

Vocabulary

- Currency
- Accept
- Commission
- Charge
- Plus tax
- Percent

- Currency exchange bureau
- Check
- Cost
- Change money
- Including tax
- Souvenir

Key Phrases

Employee:

How much would you like to change?

We charge a 1.5% commission.

How would you like to pay?

Can I have your credit card, please?

Can you sign here, please? (May I have your signature, please?)

That comes to …

Customer:

Excuse me, is there a currency exchange bureau nearby?

I'd like to change _____ into _____, please.

How much is this?   (It is $_____)

           … are these?   (They are $_____)

Can I pay by cash?

           …by credit card.

           …by travelers check(cheque).

           …by debit card.

Dialogue

Currency exchange bureau

1

Officer	Good morning
Customer	Hi, I'd like to change some money, please.

Officer	No problem sir. How much would you like to change?
Customer	Can I change $100 US to Korean Won, please?

Officer	Sure, but we charge a 1.5% commission. Is that okay?
Customer	Yes, that's fine.

Officer	Alright, that comes to 98,500 Won
Customer	Great, thank you.

Officer	Thank you, have a nice day.

Souvenir Shopping

2

Customer	Excuse me, can you tell me how much these T-shirts are?
Salesperson	Yes, they're 12 dollars each plus tax.

Customer	Okay, I'll take 2, please.
Salesperson	Certainly, what size would you like sir?

Customer	I'd like 1 large and 1 medium, please.
Salesperson	Okay, that comes to $27.60. How would you like to pay?

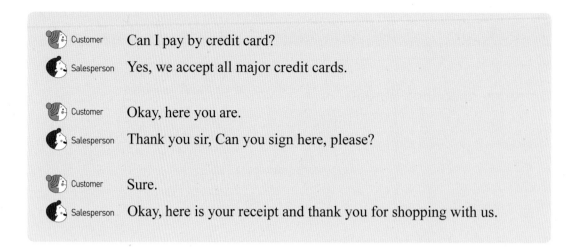

Customer	Can I pay by credit card?
Salesperson	Yes, we accept all major credit cards.
Customer	Okay, here you are.
Salesperson	Thank you sir, Can you sign here, please?
Customer	Sure.
Salesperson	Okay, here is your receipt and thank you for shopping with us.

 Activity

Using the words from the vocabulary section at the beginning of the unit.
Fill in the blanks.

1. We charge a 3% _____.

2. Do you _____ travelers checks?

3. What is the _____ in Singapore?

4. Is there a _____ near here?

5. That book costs $14.99 plus _____.

6. I need to buy a _____ for my mother.

More Practice:

Work in pairs and try to think of as many countries and currencies as you can. When you are finished, discuss as a class then fill in the chart below.

Country	Currency
	Baht
Singapore	
Japan	
	Won
Mexico	
	Euro
Indonesia	
	Yuan
Canada	
Philippines	

Creative thinking:

In partners, use the clues below and the key phrases from the beginning of the chapter to make up a dialogue and then practice reading it together.

	Customer	Clerk
1	Ask the clerk how much the postcards are	Tell customer they are each $1 plus tax
2	Tell her you will take 10 and ask how much is the total	Tell him the total is $11.50
3	Ask if the store accepts credit card	Say no, only cash or travelers check
4	Say you will pay by cash	Thank customer

Listening 1

Listen to the *dialogue* and fill in the blanks

Person 1   Good afternoon, ma'am. How may I help you?

Person 2   Yes, I'd like to _____ some money, please.

Person 1   Sure, how much _____ like to change?

Person 2   I'd like to change 1,000 _____ into US Dollars please.

Person 1   We charge a 3% _____. Is that okay?

Person 2   Yes, that's fine.

Person 1   Okay, that _____ 785.50 US Dollars.

Person 2   Thank you.

Person 1   Thank you, have a nice day.

Amusement Parks

Amusement Parks

Goals

- You will be able to answer questions about amusement park times, cost and location.
- You will be able to make safety requests politely.

- Rides
- Parade
- Roller coaster
- Wrist band
- Season pass
- Refreshments
- Lockers
- Secure
- Safety belt
- Line up
- Souvenir shop

- Performance/show
- Fireworks show
- Ticket
- Ticket booth
- Day pass
- Lost-and-found
- Locked
- Safety bar
- Harness
- Park Guide/map

Practice

Look at the pictures and write the vocabulary word.

1. _____   2. _____   3. _____

Key Phrases

Can I see your ticket? Sure, here you are.

How long is the wait? It's about 20 minutes.

What time (when) does the parade start? It starts at 8:00 p.m.

Where is the rollercoaster? Here, I'll give you an English Park Guide.

How much is a season pass? It's 30,000 Won per person

Please hold onto the safety bar.

Please make sure you secure your personal

belongings.

Please make sure your harness is securely locked.

More Practice

Fill in the blanks with the correct word. Then select the best answer.

| When | Where | How long | How much | What time |

1	_____ is a day pass?	A	It's 35 minutes.
2	_____ does the dolphin show start?	B	It closes at 11:00 p.m.
3	_____ does the park close?	C	It's 35,000 Won
4	_____ is the wait?	D	It starts at noon.
5	_____ is the souvenir shop?	E	It's near the ticket booth. Here is a map.

Listening 1

Listen to the *conversation* and answer the questions.

1. What is the name of the amusement park?

   _____

2. What show does the customer want to see?

   _____

3. How much is the show?

   _____

4. What time does the show start?

   _____

5. How long does the show last?

   _____

6. Where is the show?

   _____

Activity

Look at the flier. With your partner ask and answer questions about the amusement park. Then, plan your own flier for an amusement park. Think of a theme, costs, special events and slogans for your theme park.

Safari World
Where the jungle is all for you

Explore the safari and have the best thrills
and excitement

Open daily from 9 a.m. until 10 p.m.
Daily Elephant parade starts at the Jungle Rollercoaster

"It's more than a zoo, it's an
adventure"

Admission: 20,000 Won. Children under 12 free.

International Cultures

Appendix A

International Cultures

Australia

Country Background

Language

English is the official language of Australia; it is spoken by 95 percent of the population. Australian grammar and spelling are a mix of British and American patterns. For example, labor (American spelling) and labour (British spelling).

Religion

Christians, divided equally between Anglicans and Roman Catholics, make up 76 percent of the population. Jews, Muslims, and Buddhists are also present.

Demographics

Australia has a population of 25.2 million, concentrated mainly on the southern and eastern coasts. The 206,000 aboriginals constitute only 1.2 percent of the Australian population. Immigration continues to be largely from Europe although significant numbers are arriving from Asia.

Business Practices

Appointments

- Be punctual at meetings. To Australian business people, tardiness signals a careless business attitude.
- Business hours are 9:00 a.m. to 5:00 p.m., Monday through Friday and 9:00 a.m. to noon, Saturdays.

Business Entertaining

- Australians do not make unannounced visits; always call ahead.
- Australians do not invite strangers into their homes right away. They take their time getting to know someone before an invitation is made.
- To avoid confusion, remember that "afternoon tea" is around 4:00 p.m., "tea" is the evening meal served between 6:00 and 8:00 p.m., and "supper" is a late-night snack.
- Australians respect people with opinions, even if those opinions conflict with their own. Arguments are considered entertaining, so do not be shy about expressing any truly held beliefs.

Protocol

Greetings

- Australians are friendly and easy to get to know.
- Australians greet each other with "Hello" or an informal "G'day."
- It is the custom to shake hands at the beginning and end of a meeting.

● It is appropriate to present a business card at an introduction, but don't be surprised if you do not get one in return since many Australians do not have them.

Gestures

● The thumbs-up sign which usually signifies hitchhiking or "Okay" is considered rude.
● For a man to wink at a woman, even when being friendly is inappropriate.

Dress

● Dress is generally informal.
● Business dress is conservative.

Gifts

● Australians do not generally give gifts in a business context. If you are invited to a home for dinner, however, you may want to bring a small gift of flowers, wine, chocolates or folk crafts from home.
● As a foreigner, an illustrated book from your home area makes a good gift.

Canada

Country Background

Language

English and French are the official languages, with French predominately in Quebec.

Religion

The traditional division of Canada between Roman Catholic and Protestant remains. Jews and Eastern Orthodox each constitute less than 2 percent.

Demographics

The current population of Canada is about 36.95 million. The traditional French and British lineage of Canadians has been changed by immigration and inter-marriage. Twentieth-century immigrants were likely to be German, Italian or Ukrainian. The return of the British Hong Kong colony to mainland Chinese control in 1997 has prompted many Hong Kong Chinese to come to Canada. Native Americans and Inuits constitute only 1.5 percent of Canada's population.

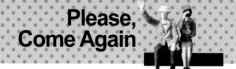

Business Practices

Appointments

- People in many countries write the day first, then the month, then the year. December 3, 1999 is written 3.12.99. This is usually the case in Canada.
- Mornings tend to be preferred for appointments.

Business Entertaining

- Business meals are popular in Canada, although the concept of breakfast meeting is only now gaining acceptance.
- Most entertaining is done in public establishments such as restaurants.
- Traditionally dinners were considered social occasions.
- Invitations to dine at home are relatively infrequent.

Protocol

Greetings

- The standard greeting is a smile, often accompanied by a nod, wave, and/or verbal greeting.
- In business situations, a handshake is used upon greetings or introductions.
- Good friends and family members sometimes embrace, especially among the French.
- If you see an acquaintance at a distance, a wave is appropriate.
- The greeting "How are you?" is not an inquiry about your health. The best response is a short one, such as "Fine, thanks." or "I'm okay."

Gestures

- The standard space between you and your conversation partner should be two feet. British Canadians are uncomfortable standing any closer to another person.
- To beckon someone, wave all fingers in a scooping motion with the palm facing up.
- Direct eye contact shows that you are sincere.
- In business situations, maintain good posture and a less casual pose.

Dress

- In cities, conservative business attire is best.
- In rural areas and small towns, clothing is less formal and less fashionable.
- When not working, Canadians dress casually.

Gifts

- Business gifts should be modest.
- When you visit a home, it is customary to take a gift. Flowers, candy, or alcohol are common gifts.
- A good time to give a gift is when you arrive or when you leave.
- Business gifts are given after you close a deal.
- Taking someone out for a meal or other entertainment is a common gift.

China

Country Background

Language

The official language is standard Chinese, based on the Mandarin dialect. It is spoken by more than 70 percent of the population. Many Chinese speak Cantonese, Wu and Keija dialects. English is spoken by many business people.

Religion

Although the government encourages atheism, the Chinese constitution guarantees religious freedom. Buddhism, Islam, and Christianity are the three major formal religions practiced in China.

Demographics

China has 1.4 billion inhabitants making it the most populous country in the world. One quarter of the earth's population lives there. Although there are many minority groups, over 91 percent of the population is ethnic (Han) Chinese.

Business Practices

Appointments

- It is very important to be punctual in China, not only for business meetings, but for social occasions as well. Lateness or cancellation is a serious offence.

Business Entertaining

- Business lunches have become more popular. One should always return the favor.
- If you are a guest, always arrive promptly or even a little early.
- Never begin to eat or drink before your host does.
- When eating rice, it is customary to hold the bowl close to your mouth.
- The Chinese use chopsticks for eating and a porcelain spoon for soup.
- Try not to drop your chopsticks, it is considered bad luck.
- Serving dishes are not passed around. It is acceptable to reach in front of others to get to the serving dishes.
- The serving of fruit signals the end of the meal.
- If you don't want refills of tea, leave some in your cup.

Protocol

Greetings

- The Chinese nod or bow slightly when greeting another person, Although handshakes are common. Wait for the Chinese to extend a hand first.

Gestures

- Avoid making exaggerated gestures or using dramatic facial expressions.
- The Chinese do not like to be touched by people they do not know.
- Members of the same sex may be seen publicly holding hands, but public affection between the opposite sexes is not condoned.
- Do not put your hands in your mouth. Biting your nails, dislodging food from your teeth etc. is considered disgusting.

Dress

- For business, men should wear conservative suits, shirts, and ties. Loud colors are not appropriate.
- Casual wear is still somewhat conservative.

Gifts

- Gift giving is a sensitive issue in China.
- Avoid giving anything of value in front of others, as it could cause the recipient both embarrassment and trouble.

England

Country Background

Language

English is the official language of England.

Religion

England has an official religion, the Anglican church, or Church of England. Most English belong to this church, which was founded when England split from the Roman Catholic church during the reign of King Henry VIII. The church no longer has political power. Religion is considered to be a very private subject.

Demographics

The population of the United Kingdom is 66 million. London, the capital has about 8.7 million in its metropolitan area. England is an urbanized and suburbanized nation, and has one of the highest population densities in the world.

Business Practices

Appointments

- Always be punctual in London. Traffic can make this difficult, so allow plenty of time to get to your appointment.
- Schedule your visits at least a few days ahead of time, and then confirm your appointment upon your arrival in England.
- Change is not necessarily a good thing in England.
- The English are normally more interested in short-term results than in the long-term future.
- Decision making is slower in England than in the United States.
- The English do not consider themselves European.
- Avoid controversial topics such as politics or religion, and do not discuss the English work ethic.
- Speak in complete sentences. Starting a sentence and then allowing it to trail off without ever completing the thought can be annoying to the English.
- Do not make jokes about the royal family.
- The English usually enjoy talking about animals.

Business Entertaining

- Business breakfasts are not common place in England.
- Breakfasts in hotels are very large.
- When passing items around the table, always pass them to the left.
- Always keep your hands above the table. Keep your elbows off the table.
- Maintain very proper manners.
- The English still respect the tradition of men holding doors open for women and rising when women enter the room.

Protocol

Greetings

- A handshake is standard for business occasions and when visiting a home.
- Women do not necessarily shake hands.
- When introduced, say 'How do you do?" instead of "Nice to meet you."

Gestures

- It is considered rude to talk with one's hands in one's pockets.
- The British often do not look at the other person while they talk.
- Don't point with your fingers, but instead indicate something with your head.
- Sitting with your ankle resting on your knee may be seen as impolite.
- It is inappropriate to touch others in public.
- The English maintain a wide physical space between conversation partners.
- Avoid excessive hand gestures when speaking.

Dress

- Conservative dress is very important.
- Men should wear laced shoes, not loafers.
- Men's shirts should not have pockets; if they do, the pockets should be empty.
- Women should also dress conservatively.

Gifts

- Gifts are not part of doing business in England.
- Rather than giving gifts, it is preferable to invite your hosts out for a meal or a show.
- Be cautious in making purchases, as there is usually no refund or exchange policy.

France

Country Background

Language

French is the official language. The French people are very proud of their language, which was the international language of diplomacy for centuries. If you do not speak French, it is advisable to apologize for this. However, many French business people speak English.

Religion

There is no official religion. France is principally a Catholic country.

Demographics

The population of France is 65.3 million. Urbanization occurred after World War II, and now cities are home to 75 percent of the people. 10.5 million people live in Paris and the surrounding suburbs.

Business Practices

Appointments

- Always make appointments for both business and social occasions. Always be punctual, although in the south the French are more relaxed about time.
- Most French get four or five weeks of summer vacation and take it in July and August.
- Eye contact among the French is frequent and intense.
- The French are known for their formal and reserved nature.
- Hierarchies are strict.
- Women should not mistake French gallantry for condescension.
- Don't start a conversation by asking personal questions.
- Don't mistake a high-pitched voice and excited gestures for anger; they usually just mean great interest in the subject.
- The French are very formal in their letter-writing style

Business Entertaining

- Business can be conducted during any meal, but lunch is best.
- Lunch can last two hours. Dinner is late (8:00 or 9:00 p.m.).
- Whoever initiates the meal or drink is expected to pay.
- Reservations are necessary in most restaurants.
- The French have a great appreciation for good conversationalists.
- When eating, keep both hands on the table at all times.
- Wine is customary with meals. If you do not want any, turn your glass upside down before the meal.
- Respect privacy. The French close doors behind them; you should do the same. Knock and wait before entering.

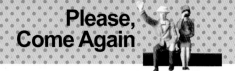

Please, Come Again

Protocol

Greetings
- Always shake hands when being introduced or when meeting someone, as well as when leaving.
- In social settings, with friends touching cheeks and kissing the air is common.

Gestures
- Don't chew gum in public.
- Men should stand up or make a move to stand up when a visitor or a superior enters the room

Dress
- The French are very aware of dress. Be conservative and wear dark suits.
- French suits are cut differently to the North American style.

Gifts
- Don't give a business gift at your first encounter.
- Good taste is extremely important with gifts.
- Good gifts include books or music, as they show interest in the intellect.

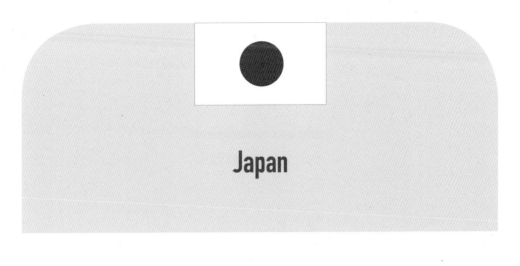

Japan

Country Background

Language

Japanese is the official language of Japan. It is a complex and subtle language and is spoken nowhere else in the world as a primary tongue. Most sentences in Japanese can be expressed on at least four different levels of politeness. Communication in Japan is often marked by great subtlety; information is left unspoken yet is perfectly understood.

Religion

The Shinto religion is unique to Japan. The institution of the emperor is supported by Shintoism. However, the Japanese are very tolerant of religious differences and may even practice both Buddhism and Shinto concurrently.

Demographics

Japan's population approaches 127.0 million. This dense population is cited as the prevailing factor explaining the Japanese "group mentality." The land represents only 0.3 percent of the world's land mass, yet its people represent

3 percent of the world's population. In these conditions, conformity and group activity have proved to be the best way to avoid conflict.

Business Practices

Appointments

- Be punctual at all times.
- A Japanese response "I'll consider it" may actually mean "no."
- "Connections" are very helpful in Japan.
- Because age equals rank, show the greatest respect to the oldest members of the Japanese group with whom you are in contact.
- The Japanese will not explain exactly what is expected of you.
- Do not make accusation or refuse anything directly; be indirect.
- On the job, the Japanese are very serious and do not try to "lighten things up" with humor.

Business Entertaining

- Business entertaining usually occurs after business hours and very rarely in the home.
- When you are taken out, your host will treat.
- If you are invited to a Japanese home, keep in mind that this is a great honor, and you should show great appreciation.
- Never point your chopsticks at another person. When you are not using them, you should line them up on the chopstick rest.
- Use both hands to hold a bowl or cup that you wish to be refilled.
- Eventually you will wish to invite your hosts out. Be insistent, even if they claim that a foreigner should not pay for anything. It is best to choose a Western-style restaurant for this occasion.

Protocol

Greetings

- The Japanese are very aware of Western habits, and will often greet you with a handshake.
- The bow is their traditional greeting.

Gestures

- Avoid excessive arm and hand movements, unusual facial expressions, or dramatic gestures of any kind.
- Pointing is considered impolite.
- The Japanese do not approve of male-female touching in public.
- Men do not engage in backslapping or other forms of touching.
- In conversation, the Japanese remain farther apart than do North Americans.
- Direct eye contact is not the norm.
- Silence is not uncomfortable for the Japanese, it is considered useful.

Dress

- Men should wear conservative suits, and never appear casual.
- Women should dress conservatively, keeping jewelry, perfume, and makeup to a minimum.
- In summer it is very hot in Japan, so bring cotton clothes. Be sure to have enough changes of clothes, because the Japanese are very concerned with neatness.
- If you wear a kimono, wrap it left over the right side! Only corpses wear them wrapped right over left.

Gifts

- Gift giving is very common in Japan.
- For the Japanese, the ceremony of gift giving is more important than the objects exchanged.
- The Japanese do not usually open gifts directly upon receiving them.
- Always wrap your gifts while in Japan or have them wrapped by a hotel or store service.
- Avoid giving gifts made up of even numbers, such as an even number of flower in a bouquet. Four is a number that should be avoided, as it is associated with death.

Philippines

Country Background

Religion

Approximately 83 percent of Filipinas profess to be Roman Catholic, but traditional beliefs remain strong.

Demographics

Today 104 million Filipinas live an urban and rural life. 43 percent live in the cities, 57 percent in the country. The population of Manila, the capital and largest city, is about 13.4 million.

Business Practices

Appointments

● Foreigners are expected to be on time for all business appointments.

Filipinas tend to be reasonably punctual for business meetings.

● Most Filipina social events do not begin at the stated time. Therefore it would be impolite to arrive on time to a party. The more important the guests, the later they are expected to arrive. This could range from fifteen minutes to as much as two hours late.

● English is the language of most business transactions and virtually all business or government correspondence in the Philippines.

Business Entertaining

● Filipinas smile constantly. However smiles and laughter do not necessarily indicate happiness or amusement.

● Filipinas may smile or laugh in situations that Westerners consider inappropriate. Smiles hide embarrassment and discord. A Filipina doctor may smile while telling a patient he is seriously ill.

● Filipinas consider everyone is worthy of respect.

● Speak in quiet, gentle tones. Filipinas like harmony.

● Once you become accepted, Filipinas are very sociable and love to talk.

● Food is vitally important in Filipina culture. Social occasions always involve food.

Protocol

Greetings

● Foreign businessmen should expect to shake hands firmly with Filipina men, both upon introduction and at subsequent meetings.

● Traditionally there is no physical contact between men and women in public.

● Close female friends in the Philippines hug and kiss upon greeting.

Gestures

● Due to the past U.S. military presence in the Philippines, most North American gestures are recognized.

● Pointing can be easily taken for an insulting gesture.

● Staring in the Philippines has a usually negative nuance.

● Do not stand with your hands on your hips. It is always interpreted as an aggressive posture.

Dress

● Because it is hot and humid in the Philippines, Filipina business dress is often casual. Dark trousers and white short-sleeved shirts for men and white long-sleeved blouses and skirts for women.

● As a foreigner, you should dress more conservatively until you are sure what degree of formality is expected.

● Many Filipina men wear an embroidered shirt called a barong.

● Neither men nor women should wear shorts or sandals in public, except at the beach.

Gifts

● Gift giving is an important part of Filipina society. Flowers and food are the most common gifts.

● When invited to a Filipina home, bring flowers, candy or chocolates to your hostess.

Singapore

Country Background

Language

Singapore has four official languages: Malay, Tamil, Chinese and English. To unify Singapore's three fractious ethnic groups English became the language of instruction, business and government.

Religion

Most of the indigenous Malay are Muslim but not all Muslims are Malay. The Muslims account for over 15 percent of the population. Similarly, Christianity is adhered to by several different ethnic groups. Wisely, Singapore has no official religion.

Demographics

Almost 5.79 million people live in this tiny nation. As a prosperous trading center, Singapore attracted many races. The vast majority of Singaporeans are Chinese.

144

Business Practices

Appointments

- It is important to be on time for all business appointments.
- English is the language of most business transactions.
- Since politeness demands that a Singaporean not disagree openly, the word "no" is rarely heard. A polite but evasive "yes" is simply a technique to avoid giving offense. In Singapore, "yes" can mean anything from "I agree" to "maybe" to "I hope you can tell from my lack of enthusiasm that I really mean 'no'."
- Politeness is the single most important attribute for successful relationships in Singapore.
- People in Singapore may smile or laugh in situations that Westerners consider inappropriate.
- In Singapore, one who expresses anger in public has shamefully lost face. Such a person will not be trusted or respected.
- Age and seniority are highly respected.
- Speak in quiet, gentle tones. Always remain calm. Leave plenty of time for someone to respond to a statement you make.
- Good topics for discussion include tourism, travel, plans for the future, organizational success.

Business Entertaining

Food is vitally important in Singapore culture. Social occasions always involve food.

Take advantage of any invitations to social events. Establishing a successful business relationship hinges on establishing a social relationship as well.

Singapore's anti-corruption laws are so strict that government officials may be prohibited from attending social events.

Protocol

Greetings

- Singapore has three major ethnic groups, each with its own traditions: Chinese, Malay and Indian.
- With younger or foreign-educated Singaporeans, a handshake is the most common form of greeting.
- In Singapore, Westernized women may shake hands with both men and women.
- The traditional Malay greeting is called the salaam, which is akin to a handshake without a grip. Both parties stretch out one or both hands, touch each other's hand(s) lightly, then bring their hand(s) back to rest over their heart.
- Many, but not all Singaporean Indians are Hindu. They avoid public contact between men and women. Men may shake hands with men, and women with women, but only Westernized Hindus will shake hands with the opposite sex.
- The traditional Indian greeting involves a slight bow with the palms of the hands together.

Gestures

- Aside from handshakes, there is no public contact between the sexes in Singapore. Do not kiss or hug a person of the opposite sex in public.
- Among both Muslims and Hindus, the left hand is considered unclean. Eat with your right hand only. Do not touch anything or anyone with your left hand if you can use your right hand instead.
- The foot is also considered unclean. Do not move anything with your feet, and do not touch anything with your feet.

- It is impolite to point at anyone with the forefinger. Malays use a forefinger only to point to animals.
- The head is considered the seat of the soul by many Indians and Malays. Never touch someone's head, not even to pat the hair of a child.

Dress

- Singapore is only some 136.8 kilometers north of the Equator. It is hot and humid all year long, with a temperature range of 24-31 degrees Celsius, and humidity above 90 percent.
- Because of the heat and humidity, business dress in Singapore is often casual.

Gifts

- Singapore prides itself on being the most corruption-free state in Asia.
- The Chinese traditionally decline a gift three times before accepting: this prevents them from appearing greedy. Continue to insist: once they accept the gift, say that you are pleased that they have done so.

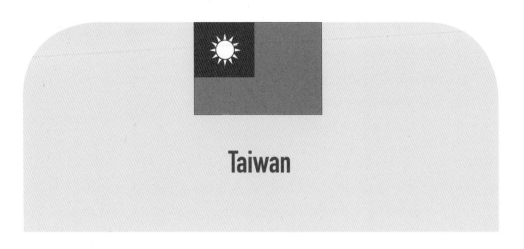

Taiwan

Country Background

Language

The official language of Taiwan is traditional Mandarin Chinese, although Taiwanese is spoken more and more frequently. The Taiwanese do not use the modernized Chinese script currently used in the People's Republic of China. English is a popular language to study in school and many business representatives can speak, understand, and correspond in English.

Religion

The religious distribution is 93 percent Buddhist, Confucian, and Taoist; 4.5 percent Christian; and 2.5 percent other religions.

Demographics

Taiwan's population of 23.7 million is primarily Taiwanese and mainland Chinese. Only 2 percent of the population consists of the aboriginal inhabitants of Taiwan.
Almost 55 percent of Taiwanese are under age thirty.

Business Practices

Appointments

- Be punctual to all appointments. This is expected from foreigners and is a sign of good manners.
- Traffic in Taiwan is very congested. Unless your next appointment is so close that you can get there on foot, plan for long travel times between appointments.

Business Entertaining

- Hospitality is very, very important. Expect to be invited out many times after work.
- Never visit a home unannounced.
- Good topics of conversation include Chinese sights, art, calligraphy, family, and inquiries about the health of the other's family.

Protocol

Greetings

- When meeting someone for the first time, a nod of the head is sufficient. When meeting friends or acquaintances, a handshake is appropriate. Show respect by bowing slighty with your hands at your sides and your feet together.
- Elderly people are very highly respected, so it is polite to speak with them first. Don't be surprised if you are asked if you have eaten. This is a common greeting originating during the famines of feudal times. This phrase is comparable with "How are you?" in the West. A polite response is

"yes," even if you have not eaten.

● Wait to be introduced to another at gatherings and parties.

Gestures

● Do not wink at a person, even in friendship.

● Do not put your arm around another's shoulders.

● Do not touch the head of another person's child. Children are considered precious, and it is believed that they may be damaged by careless touching.

● Chinese point with their open hands, since pointing with a finger is considered rude.

Dress

Dress modestly for casual activities

Gifts

● When giving or receiving a gift, use both hands. The gift is not opened in the presence of the giver.

● The Chinese associate all of the following with funerals – do not give them as gifts:

Straw sandals

Clocks

A stork or a crane

Handkerchiefs

Gifts (or wrapping paper) where the predominant color is white, black, or blue.

● Also avoid any gifts of knives, scissors, or cutting tools; to the Chinese, they suggest the severing of a friendship.

United States of America (U.S.A.)

Country Background

Language

English is the official language. Spanish is the most widely used second language.

Religion

Church and state have always been separate in the United States; however over three-quarters of U.S. citizens belong to a religious group. Most are Christian. Judaism and Islam each account for about 2 percent of the population.

Demographics

The population of the United States is about 327.16 million. The largest city is New York, which has over 8.2 million people within its boundaries, and more in its surrounding area.

Business Practices

Appointments

- Punctuality is highly emphasized. If you are invited you should arrive promptly.
- People in the United States write the month first, then the day, then the year; for example December 3, 2007 is written 12/3/07.
- Prior appointments are necessary.
- Many convenience stores are open twenty-four hours.

Business Entertaining

- When eating out, the cost can be shared with friends. This is called "splitting the bill," "getting separate checks," or "going Dutch."
- Before going to visit a friend, you must call ahead.
- Most parties are informal, unless the hosts tell you otherwise.
- If you are offered food or drink, you are not obliged to accept. Also, your host will probably not urge you to eat, so help yourself whenever you want.
- Many foods are eaten with the hands; take your lead from others, or if you are uncomfortable, do as you like.
- It is not considered rude to eat while walking; many people also eat in their cars (even while driving).

Protocol

Greetings

- The standard greeting is a smile, often accompanied by a nod, wave, and/or verbal greeting.
- In business situations, a handshake is used.
- Good friends and family members usually embrace, finishing the embrace with a pat or two on the back.
- In casual situations a smile and verbal greeting is adequate.
- If you see an acquaintance at a distance, a wave is appropriate.
- The greeting "How are you?" is not an inquiry about your health. The best response is a short one, such as "Fine, thanks." or "I'm alright."

Gestures

- The standard space between you and your conversation partner should be about two feet.
- In general, friends of the same sex do not hold hands.
- The slap on the back is a sign of friendship.
- To wave good-bye, move your entire hand, palm facing outward.
- Direct eye contact shows that you are sincere, although it should not be too intense. Some minorities look away to show respect.
- When giving an item to another person, one may toss it or hand it over with only one hand.

Dress

- In cities, conservative business attire is best.

- In rural areas and small towns, clothing is less formal and less fashionable.
- When not working, dress casually.
- If you wish to wear traditional clothing from your country, feel free to do so.

Gifts

- Business gifts are discouraged by the law.
- When you visit a home, it is not necessary to take a gift; however it is always appreciated. You may take flowers, a plant, or a bottle of wine.
- If you stay in a U.S. home for a few days, a gift is appropriate. You should also write a letter of thanks.
- When staying in a U.S. home you will probably be expected to help out around the house by making your bed, helping to clear the dishes after a meal, and so forth.
- A good time to give a gift is when you arrive or when you leave. The best gifts are those that come from your country.
- Taking someone out for a meal or other entertainment is a common gift.

호주

역사

호주의 첫 이주자는 원주민 애버리진의 조상으로서 3만 8000년 이전에 동남아시아 방면에서 이주해 왔다.

호주는 1606년 내항한 얀스에서 1642년, 1646년에 내항한 네덜란드인 항해자와 1688년에 내항한 영국인에 의해서 대륙 북부해안과 서부연안 및 태즈메이니아 섬 남쪽기슭의 해안선이 알려지게 되었다. 그러나 인도네시아로부터 북쪽해안에 이르는 해상어로를 제외하고는 19세기로 접어들 때까지 호주는 미지의 땅이었다.

호주가 식민 지배가 가능한 토지라는 사실은 1770년 대륙 동쪽해안을 조사한 영국 해군 제임스 쿡에 의하여 알려졌다. 1788년 1월 26일 현재의 시드니 땅에 상륙한 약 1,000여명의 유형자와 군인에 의해 유형 식민지가 만들어졌다. 영국의 영유범위는 점차 확대되어 1827년 대륙 전체가 영국령이 되었다.

1840년대까지는 호주가 자유식민지로 전환하는 시기였다. 1820년대에 들면서 군정이 끝나고 자유이민의 증가가 두드러지게 나타났다. 지리적으로는 연안 각지 및 내륙 조사가 진행되어 현재의 각 주도에 대한 입식이 시작되면서 식민지의 기초가 구축되었다.

1850~1890년대는 식민지경제의 자립과 발전기였다. 1850년대에는 동부 5개 식민지, 1890년 웨스턴 오스트레일리아가 선거에 의한 의회와 내각책임제를 도입하면서 자치식민지가 되었다.

1900년대~제2차 세계대전에는 1901년 연방 결성에 의한 정치적 자립과 국내 통일을 배경으로 이민·관세·노동·사회보장 등에 관한 독자적 정책 및 제도가 형성되었다.

제2차 세계대전 후 호주는 대외 관계의 변화와 함께 미국과의 유대를 너욱 상화하였으며 영국으로부터 상대적인 이탈이 진행되었다. 현재 호주는 동남아시와의 관계 회복에 힘쓰고 있다.

언어

호주의 공식 언어는 영어이다. 인구의 95%가 영어를 사용하고 있다. 호주 문법과 철자는 미국식과 영국식이 섞여있다. 예를 들어 미국식으로는 노동을 labor로 쓰지만 영국식으로는 labour로 쓴다.

종교

총 인구의 75%가 기독교를 믿는다. 이는 영국 성공회와 로마 천주교로 골고루 나누어져 있다. 유태교, 회교도 그리고 불교 신자도 있다.

인구통계

호주는 2억 5천 2백만의 인구가 있으며 이들은 남부 해안과 동부 해안에 집중적으로 살고 있다. 20만 6천에 이르는 원주민은 호주 인구의 1.2% 밖에 되지 않는다. 주로 유럽에서 호주로 이민자들이 많이 유입되고 있으며 아시아에서도 상당수의 이민자가 호주로 이주하고 있다.

비즈니스 관행

약속

- 회의 시간은 반드시엄수 해야 한다. 호주 비즈니스맨들에게는 시간을 지키지 못하는 것은 무성의한 비즈니스 태도로 인식될 수 있다.
- 업무 시간은 월요일부터 금요일까지는 오전 9시부터 오후 5시, 토요일은 오전 9시에서 12시까지 이루어진다.

비즈니스 접대

- 호주인들은 사전 연락 없이 방문하는 경우가 드물다. 방문을 할 경우 항상 사전에 연락해서 약속을 하도록 한다.
- 호주인들은 초면에 낯선 사람을 집으로 초대하는 경우가 드물다. 그들은 누군가를 초대 하기 전에 상대방과 친숙해지는데 충분한 시간을 갖는다.
- 혼선을 피하기 위해 'afternoon tea'는 오후 4시경이고 "tea"는 오후 6시와 8시 사이에 제공되는 저녁 식사이며 "supper"는 저녁 늦은 시간에 먹는 간식임을 기억해야 한다.
- 호주인들은 개인적 의견이 있는 사람들을 존중한다. 설사 그런 의견이 자신들의 생각과 상반되는 것이라 할지라도 토론을 즐기기 때문에 자신의 의견을 표현하는 것을 주저할 필요가 없다.

의전

인사

- 호주인들은 친절하며 쉽게 친해질 수 있다.
- 호주인들은 서로 "Hello" 또는 "Good day(G'day)"라고 인사를 나눈다.
- 회의 시작과 종료 후 악수를 하는 것이 일반적이다.
- 첫 만남이나 회의 때 명함을 상대에게 주는 것은 적절한 인사이다. 그러나 호주인들은 명함이 없는 경우가 많기 때문에 반드시 자신의 명함을 주지 않는 경우도 종종 있다는 점을 인식해야 한다.

몸 동작

- 주먹을 쥔 채 엄지손가락을 올리는 thumbs-up 신호는 통상 히치하이킹이나 Okay라는 뜻으로 이해되지만 호주에서는 매우 무례한 손짓이다.
- 남성이 여성에게 윙크하는 것은 부적절하다. 설사 그것이 친근감의 표시라 하더라도.

캐나다

역사

캐나다가 세상에 알려진 것은 10세기 경 노르만인에 의해서이며, 14세기 전반까지는 덴마크인이 거주하였으나 그 후 소멸하였다. 1497년 당시 소수의 인디언이 살고 있던 캐나다에는 영국의 헨리 7세가 진출을 꾀하고 있었으며 1628년 노바스코샤 식민지의 설립과 동시에 캐나다에 대한 영국의 진출이 본격적으로 시작되었다. 그 뒤 150년간 뉴펀들랜드, 뉴브런즈윅, 프린스에드워드섬, 그리고 허드슨만 지방에 많은 식민지가 만들어졌다. 캐나다에 대한 프랑스 진출은 1608년부터 세인트로렌스강 연안에 퀘벡·몬트리올 등의 식민지 설립을 통해 전개되었다. 영국·프랑스 양 식민지간의 투쟁은 1756~1763년간의 7년 전쟁으로 이어졌으며 퀘벡·몬트리올을 점령한 영국군의 승리로 끝났다. 7년 전쟁은 1763년의 파리조약을 체결케 했고 그 결과 캐나다는 영국의 식민지 지배를 받게 되었다.

한편, 아메리카에서 쫓겨난 구 아메리카 식민지의 제국왕당파 등의 보수분자가 아메리카에서 쫓겨나 노바스코샤주·온타리오주 등으로 이주하여 그 지역의 지배층을 형성하였다. 1849년 캐나다의 자치가 인정되어 1867년 '영국령 북아메리카 조례'에 따라 오타와를 수도로 자치연방부를 구성하였다.

1926년의 영국국제국회의는 캐나다 및 기타 자치령의 완전자치를 인정하였고, 1931년 웨스트민스터 조례에 의하여 주권국가로서 영연방을 구성하는 것이 법제화되었다.

1949년에 캐나다 헌법인 '영국령 북아메리카 조례'가 수정되어 캐나다의 완전독립이 법적으로 완성되었으며 1951년 12월 정식 국명을 캐나다자치령에서 캐나다로 변경하였다. 1982년 4월 17일 캐나다 최초의 헌법이 선포되었고 그 결과 영연방의 일원으로 존속하기는 하나 영국과의 법적 예속 관계는 종지부를 찍고 주권국가의 면모를 갖추게 되었다.

종교

천주교와 기독교의 전통적인 구성과 분포는 캐나다에서도 동일하다. 유태교와 정통교는 2%도 채 되지 않는다.

인구통계

캐나다의 현재 인구는 약 3천 7백만 명이다. 전통적으로는 프랑스와 영국계 캐나다인들이 많았으나 이는 타 민족의 이민과 타 인종간의 결혼으로 인해 바뀌고 있다. 20세기 이민자들은 주로 독일, 이태리 그리고 우크라이나에서 캐나다로 유입되었다. 1997년에 영국령이던 홍콩 본토가 중국으로 환원되면서 많은 홍콩 중국인들이 캐나다로 이민을 왔다. 원주민과 이누이족들은 캐나다 인구의 1.5%에 불과하다.

비즈니스 관행

약속

- 여러 나라에서 날짜를 쓸 때에는 일, 월, 그리고 연도순으로 작성하는데 이는 캐나다의 경우도 동일하다. 즉 2007년 12월 3일은 3.12.07로 작성한다.
- 약속은 대체로 오전에 하는 것을 선호한다.

비즈니스 접대

- 캐나다 사람들은 비즈니스 접대를 자주한다. 그러나 조찬 회의는 최근에 이르러 비로소 조금씩 행해지고 있다.
- 대부분의 접대는 레스토랑과 같은 공공 장소에서 이루어진다.
- 전통적으로 저녁 식사를 함께 하는 것이 사교 모임이라고 생각되고 있다.
- 캐나다 가정으로 초대를 받는 것은 매우 드문 일이다.

의전

인사

- 일반적인 인사는 미소를 짓는 것 그리고 고개로 살짝 인사하는 것이나 손 흔드는 것, 그리고 말로 가벼운 인사를 하는 것이다.
- 업무 상황에서는 인사나 소개를 할 때 악수를 한다.
- 친한 친구나 가족 간에는 껴안기도 한다. 이는 특히 프랑스인들이 자주하는 인사이다.
- 아는 사람이 먼 거리에 보이면 손을 흔드는 것이 적절한 인사이다.
- "How are you?"와 같은 인사는 상대의 건강을 물어보는 것은 아니다. 따라서 가장 좋은 대답은 "Fine, thanks"와 같은 짧은 인사말이다.

몸 동작

- 대화를 나누는 사람들 간의 거리는 약 60cm 정도이다. 영국계 캐나다인들은 다른 사람들과 너무 가까이 서 있는 것을 불편하게 여긴다.
- 사람을 부를 때에는 손바닥을 위로 하고 손가락을 모아 자기 쪽으로 당기는 손짓을 하면 된다.
- 눈을 직접 맞추며 얘기하는 것은 말하는 사람이 진지하다는 표시가 된다.
- 업무적 상황에서는 자세를 바르게 하고 평상시 보다는 덜 캐주얼한 태도를 보여야한다.

복장

- 도시에서는 보수적인 비즈니스 복장이 가장 적합하다.
- 지방이나 소도시에서는 복장이 조금 더 자유롭고 디자인도 무난한 것을 선호한다.
- 캐나다인들은 업무 시간 이외에는 옷을 캐주얼하게 입는다.

선물

● 업무상 하는 선물은 검소한 것이어야 한다.

● 다른 사람의 가정을 방문할 경우에는 선물을 가져가는 것이 예의이다. 꽃이나 초콜릿 또는 술 종류가 무난하다.

● 선물을 주는 좋은 시점은 도착했을 때 또는 떠날 때이다.

● 업무상 주는 선물은 계약이 체결된 후에 주는 것이 좋다.

● 상대방을 저녁식사나 공연(오페라, 연극 등)에 초대하는 것은 일반적인 선물의 범주에 속한다.

중화인민공화국

역사

중국 최초의 국가는 은나라로 전해지며 기록으로서 중국의 역사는 주나라부터 시작된다. 기원전 1122년경부터 서기 256년까지 중국을 지배한 주나라의 정치체제는 봉건제였으며 그 당시 영토는 현재 중국의 영토와 비슷하다.

춘추전국시대에는 제후들이 전 중국의 지배권을 둘러싸고 세력 다툼을 벌였다. 춘추전국시대의 혼란을 통일한 진나라는 지방제후국을 폐지하고 강력한 중앙 정부를 수립하였다. 또한 외부의 침략을 막기 위해 만리장성을 쌓았다. 한나라는 중국과 유럽을 연결하는 육상 무역로인 비단길로 유럽과 교역 하였으나 후한 말기 권력 투쟁과 부패가 점점 심해지고 대규모 반란이 일어나 230년에 멸망 하였다. 수나라는 581년 분열된 중국을 재통일하고 통치하였다. 605년에는 양쯔강 유역과 북중국을 연결하는 대운하를 설치하였다. 수나라에 이어 당나라는 618년부터 300여 년 동안 중국을 통치하였다. 그러나 755년 안·사의 난이 일어난 이후 당나라는 점차 쇠퇴하기 시작하였고 884년까지 계속된 황소의 난으로 더욱 약화되어 907년 마침내 멸망하였다. 송나라는 진나라에 이어 또 한번의 중국 통일을 이루었고 과거제의 확립과 성리학 발달이라는 두 가지 주요한 변화가 있었다. 원나라는 1279년부터 1368년까지 중국 역사상 처음으로 중국 전역을 지배한 국가로서 외국인을 위한 법을 따로 만들 정도로 발달하였다. 원이 멸망한 후 명나라는 1644년까지 중국의 안정과 번영을 이룩했고 이로 인해 한족의 영향력은 되살아났다. 19세기 이전까지 청나라는 서양인과의 접촉을 엄격히 통제하였다. 그러나 유럽 상인들은 무역 손실을 막기 위해 중국에 아편을 들여와 팔기 시작하였다. 이는 청나라의 혼란과 영국과의 아편전쟁으로 이어져 청나라에 엄청난 손실을 불러왔다. 청나라 내에서는 1864년까지 토지의 균등 분배를 주장하는 태평천국운동이 활발하게 진행되었다. 1894년 발발한 청일전쟁은 청나라를 일본의 식민지로 전락케 했으나 1945년 일본의 패전과 함께 청나라는 해방되었다. 그 후 수립된 중화인민공화국은 1952년까지 중국에 대한 통치권을 확고히 하고 경제를 회복하는 데 힘썼다. 그 당시 중국의 강력한 정치가였던 덩샤오핑은 개혁 · 개방을 주장하며 중국의 현대화를 이끌었다. 현재 중국은 일본과 더불어 아시아의 중심으로 발달하고 있으며 전 세계가 중국의 성장에 주목하고 있다.

언어

중화인민공화국의 공식 언어는 만다린을 기초로 하는 표준 중국어이다. 이는 인구의 70% 이상이 사용하고 있는 언어이다. 중국인들 중에는 캔토니즈어나, 게이자 방언을 사용하는 사람들도 많다. 비즈니스맨 중에는 영어를 사용하는 사람들이 많다.

종교

정부는 무교를 권장하지만 중국 헌법은 종교적 자유를 보장하고 있다. 그리고 중국에 있는 가장 주요한 공식적 종교들은 불교, 회교 그리고 기독교이다.

인구통계

중국은 약 14억의 인구를 갖고 있으며 이로 인해 전 세계에서 가장 인구밀도고 높은 국가이다. 즉 지구상의 인구 중 25%가 중국에서 살고 있다는 것이다. 중국에는 다수의 소수민족이 있지만 91%는 고유 민족인 한족으로 구성되어 있다.

비즈니스 관행

약속

● 중국에서는 업무나 회의 시간뿐만 아니라 사교 모임에도 시간 약속을 지키는 것이 매우 중요하다. 약속에 늦거나 약속을 취소하는 것은 상대방에게 심한 모욕감을 주는 행위이다.

비즈니스 접대

- 중국인들 사이에는 비즈니스 점심 접대를 상당히 선호하고 있다. 점심 초대를 받았으면 답례로 상대방을 반드시 초대해 주는 것이 예의이다.
- 만약 초대를 받았다면 시간에 맞추어 또는 약간 일찍 도착해야한다.
- 주빈 (초대한 사람)이 먼저 식사를 시작하기 전에는 음식을 먹거나 음료를 마시면 안 된다.
- 공기에서 밥을 먹을 경우에는 밥공기를 입 가까이 대고 먹는 것이 일반적이다.
- 중국인들은 음식을 먹을 때에는 젓가락을 사용하고 스프나 국을 먹을 때에는 사기 수저를 사용한다.
- 젓가락을 바닥에 떨어뜨리지 않도록 주의해야한다. 젓가락을 떨어뜨리는 것은 액운으로 여긴다.
- 식사 중에는 음식이 담긴 접시를 서로 건네주는 경우가 없다. 다른 사람 앞으로 팔을 뻗어 음식 접시를 드는 것은 결례가 아니다.
- 과일이 제공되는 것은 식사가 끝났다는 신호이다.
- 차를 더 이상 마시기 싫다면 찻잔에 차를 약간 남겨두면 된다.

의전

인사

- 중국인들은 다른 사람을 만났을 때 고개를 살짝 숙이는 목례로 인사를 한다. 그러나 악수를 하는 경우도 많다. 중국인 측에서 먼저 손을 내밀어 악수를 청하기를 기다려야 한다.

몸 동작

- 과장된 몸동작이나 극적인 표정을 짓지 않도록 주의한다.
- 중국인들은 잘 모르는 사람들이 자신을 만지는 것을 싫어한다.
- 동성끼리는 공공장소에서 손을 잡는 것을 흔히 볼 수 있다. 그러나 이성간에 애정 표현을 드러내는 것은 너그럽게 봐주지 않는다.
- 손을 입에 넣는 것은 삼가야한다. 손톱을 깨무는 것이나 입에 손을 넣어 이 사이에 낀 음식을 빼는 것 등은 혐오스러운 일이다.

복장

● 업무를 보려면 남성들은 정장이나 셔츠와 넥타이를 착용해야한다. 밝고 튀는 색상은 적절하지 않다.

● 캐주얼웨어 조차에 대해서도 아직은 보수적인 성향이 있다.

선물

● 중국에서 선물을 주는 것은 아직도 매우 민감한 사안이다.

● 고가의 선물을 여러 사람 앞에서 증정하는 것은 삼가야한다. 자칫하면 받는 사람에게 수치심을 주거나 문제를 유발 시킬 수 있다.

대영제국

역사

중석기시대를 거쳐 5세기 중엽 앵글로색슨족이 대륙에서 영국으로 이주하면서 영국의 역사는 시작된다. 영국의 역사가 본격적으로 시작되는 1337년 프랑스와 프랑스의 왕위계승 문제를 둘러싼 백년전쟁이 발발하여 대부분의 대륙령을 상실하였다. 백년전쟁이 끝나고 2년 후 영국에서 왕위 계승을 둘러싼 귀족들 간의 전쟁이 일어나고 그 결과 요크 가문이 승리하여 에드워드 4세가 왕위에 오르게 된다. 1485년 왕위에 오른 헨리 7세가 절대주의 왕권의 기초를 확립하였다. 이어 헨리 8세는 이혼 문제로 로마 교황과 갈등을 일으켜 직접 교회의 수장이 되는 영국 국교회를 설립하였다. 그러나 헨리 8세의 아들 에드워드 6세에 이어 메리가 여왕으로 즉위하자 메리는 영국 국교회를 탄압하였다. 메리 여왕 이후 엘리자베스 1세는 두 종파의 갈등에서 오는 폐해를 극복하기 위해 새로이 영국 국교회를 확립하였다.

1603년 영국 왕위에 오른 제임스 1세가 왕권신수설을 주장하며 의회와 대립하였다. 1628년 의회가 권리 청원을 통과시키자 제임스 1세는 의회를 해산시켰고 결국 의회파와 왕당파 사이의 내전은 올리버 크롬웰이 이끄는 의회군에 의해 청교도 혁명으로 발전하였다. 크롬웰이 죽자 의회는 네덜란드로 망명한 찰스 2세를 맞이하여 왕정을 복귀시켰다.

찰스 2세는 국교주의의 재건에 힘쓰는 의회와 다시 마찰을 빚었다. 찰스의 뒤를 이은 제임스 2세 역시 카톨릭주의와 절대주의로 복귀하려고 하였다. 그러자 의회는 권리장전을 기반으로 네덜란드의 메리와 오렌지 공 윌리엄을 여왕과 왕으로 불러들이고 제임스는 프랑스로 망명하게 하는 명예혁명을 일으켰다.

윌리엄 3세와 그 뒤를 이은 앤 여왕의 치세 동안 영국은 주요 해상국으로 부상하였고 식민지 체제를 확대해 나갔다. 이를 바탕으로 영국은 산업 혁명이라는 비약적인 발전을 이루었다.

　　19세기 전반기에는 노동자층을 주체로 전개된 민중 운동인 차티스트 운동과 반곡물법 운동이 일어났다. 1914년 제1차 세계 대전이 발발하였고 영국은 1914년 8월 4일 선전 포고를 하였다. 제1차 세계 대전 이후 영국은 경제 불황을 겪게 되고 여러 가지 화폐 정책을 실시하였으나 실효가 없었다. 영국에게 제2차 세계대전은 제1차 세계 대전보다 더욱 피해가 큰 전쟁이었다.

　　영국은 세계대전을 겪은 후 선거에서 애틀리가 처칠을 물리치고 수상이 되었으며, 이와 같은 시기에 제국 체제에서 철수하여 인도, 미얀마, 스리랑카 등이 독립했다.

　　21세기에 들어선 영국은 현재 고든 브라운 총리의 집권이 향후 유럽정치에 대한 새로운 변화를 가져올 것이라고 기대하고 있다.

언어

영국의 공식적 언어는 영어이다.

종교

영국은 공식 종교가 있다. 즉 영국 성공회이다. 대부분의 영국인들은 성공회에 속해 있으며 이는 헨리 8세 왕 집권 시절 로마의 카톨릭교와 나누어지면서 생긴 종파이다. 교회는 더 이상 정치적 권력을 지니지 않고 있다. 종교는 매우 개인적인 사안으로 여긴다.

인구통계

영국의 인구는 6천 6백만 명이다. 수도인 런던은 도시 지역에 7백61만 명이 거주하고 있다. 영국은 도시화 및 준 도시화 국가로 세계에서 가장 인구밀도가 높은 국가 중 하나이다.

비즈니스 관행

약속

- 영국에서는 항상 약속 시간을 지켜야한다. 교통 사정으로 인해 어려울 수 있으니 도착 시간을 충분히 감안하여 이동한다.
- 2-3일 전에 약속을 미리 잡는 것이 좋다. 그리고 영국에 도착 후 약속을 다시 확인해야 한다.
- 영국에서는 변화가 구태여 좋은 것은 아니다.
- 영국인들은 장기적인 미래보다는 단기적인 결과에 관심이 더 많은 것이 일반적이다.
- 영국에서 의사결정은 미국에 비해 느리다.
- 영국인들은 자신을 유럽인으로 생각하지 않는다.
- 정치, 종교와 같이 논쟁을 불러일으키는 소재는 피한다. 또한 영국 근무 윤리에 대해 언급하지 않는다.
- 말을 할 때에는 완전한 문장으로 말하도록 한다. 문장을 시작하고 끝내지도 않은 채 질질 끌어버리는 것은 영국인들에게 신경에 거슬리는 일이다.
- 황실 가족에 대해 농담을 삼간다.
- 영국인들은 동물에 대해 얘기하는 것을 좋아한다.

비즈니스 접대

- 영국에서는 조찬 회의가 흔한 일이 아니다.
- 호텔에서의 조식은 식사의 양이 상당히 많다.
- 식사 중 음식이나 다른 것들을 상대방에게 건넬 때에는 항상 좌측으로 건네준다.
- 손은 항상 테이블 위에 올려놓는다. 팔꿈치는 절대로 테이블 위에 올려놓으면 안된다.
- 예절을 지키도록 신경 써야한다.
- 영국인들은 남성이 여성을 위해 문을 열어 주는 것과 여성이 들어오면 일어서는 것과 같은 전통을 지키고 있다.

의전

인사

● 비즈니스 상의 만남이나 개인 가정 방문 시에도 악수를 하는 것은 일반적인 일이다.

● 여성은 악수를 하지 않는 경우도 많다.

● 소개를 받았을 때에는 "Nice to meet you" 대신에 "How do you do?"가 더 적절하다.

몸 동작

● 손을 호주머니에 넣은 채 얘기하는 것은 무례한 일이다.

● 영국인들은 얘기하는 동안 상대방을 반드시 쳐다보지는 않는다.

● 손가락으로 사물이나 사람을 가리키면 안된다. 대신 머리로 가리키면 된다.

● 한 쪽 다리를 다른 쪽 다리에 올려놓는 것은 무례한 일이다. (다리를 꼬는 것과는 다름)

● 공공장소에서 사람을 만지는 것은 적절한 일이 아니다.

● 영국인들은 상대방과 얘기를 나눌 때 조금 떨어져 서서 얘기한다.

● 말할 때 손으로 과한 동작을 하는 것은 피해야한다.

복장

● 정장을 착용하는 것은 매우 중요하다.

● 남성은 간편한 신발 보다는 끈을 매는 구두를 신어야 한다.

● 남성의 셔츠는 호주머니가 없어야 한다. 만약 있다면 호주머니에는 아무것도 넣지 말아야한다.

● 여성도 정장을 입어야한다.

선물

● 선물 증정은 영국 비즈니스 관행에는 없는 일이다.

● 선물을 주기 보다는 비즈니스 상대를 저녁 식사나 공연에 초대하는 것이 더 낫다.

● 물건을 구매할 경우에는 주의를 기울여야한다. 왜냐하면 환불이나 교환 제도가 없기 때문이다.

프랑스

역사

기원전 8세기 경, 켈트족의 프랑스 이주를 거쳐 987년 프랑스 왕국이 멸망하고 카페 왕조가 성립되면서 프랑스의 역사는 시작된다.

프랑스에서는 1560년부터 1598년간 여덟 차례에 걸친 신교도와 구교도간의 종교전쟁이 일어났다. 그 결과, 1598년 앙리 4세가 신앙의 자유를 인정하는 '낭트칙령'을 발표하였고 종교적 갈등을 수습하였다. 루이 14세에 절정에 달하였던 브르봉 왕조는 루이 15세와 루이 16세에 걸쳐 점차 약화된 반면, 상업 자본주의와 계몽사상의 영향을 받은 부르주아 계급이 새로운 세력으로 대두되었다. 16세기 절대주의가 확립된 이래 여전히 수백년 동안 유지되고 있던 구제도에 대한 시민의 불만과 비판의식 또한 고조되었다. 결국, 자유와 평등이라는 이름 아래 파리의 민중이 봉기하였고 정치범 수용소인 바스티유 감옥을 습격하면서 프랑스 대혁명이 발발하였다. 프랑스 대혁명을 이끈 국민의회는 1789년 8월 26일 인권선언문을 발표하였다.

프랑스 대혁명 이후 프랑스는 여전히 혼란스러운 분위기였고 이를 틈타 나폴레옹이 1799년 12월 13일 쿠데타를 일으켜 제 1제정이 시작되었다.

제 1제정에서는 영국과 오스트리아가 프랑스에 대항하여 일곱 차례나 대 프랑스 동맹을 결성하였고 나폴레옹은 대륙 봉쇄령으로 이에 맞섰다. 하지만 에스파냐의 반 프랑스 전쟁, 러시아 원정의 패배와 독일해방전쟁에서의 열세는 1814년 나폴레옹을 엘바 섬으로 유배시켰다.

1852년 12월에 나폴레옹 3세가 황제로 즉위한 제 2제정은 국내적으로 비약적인 발전을 이루었다. 나폴레옹 3세의 몰락 후 왕당파와 공화파의 팽팽한 대립 속에서 시작된 제 3공화정은 1875년까지 과

도체제가 유지되다가 1875년 의회 우위의 내통령에 공화정이 수립됨으로써 프랑스는 100년에 걸친 단속적인 혁명 끝에 공화정 체제로 정착하게 되었다.

제1차 세계대전에서 프랑스는 초기에 수세에 밀렸으나 후반기에는 전세를 역전시키고 1918년 11월 11일 대독 휴전협정을 체결한다. 또한 제1차 세계 대전 이후 처리문제를 위한 파리강화회의도 프랑스 베르사유에서 열리게 된다. 제 2차 세계대전 이후에는 전승국의 대열에 합류하게 된다.

1958년 9월 28일 국민투표를 통하여 신 헌법안이 채택되었고 1985년 10월 4일 신헌법이 공포되었다. 1959년 1월 8일 드골이 대통령에 취임하게 되었다. 드골은 알제리 독립과 유럽공동시장(EEC)에서 중심적 역할을 하였으며 중국과도 외교관계를 수립하였다. 그러나 대대적인 학생데모와 총파업사태로 난국을 맞게 되고 결국 이러한 정치 불안은 1969년 4월 드골 대통령의 사직으로 마무리 된다. 1981년에는 사회당 출신으로는 처음으로 프랑수아 미테랑이 대통령으로 선출되었다.

현재 프랑스는 니콜라 사르코지가 대통령으로 재임하고 있으며 유럽의 전반적인 부분에 중심적인 역할을 담당하고 있다.

언어

프랑스의 공식 언어는 불어이다. 프랑스인들은 자신의 언어에 대해 자부심이 강하다. 프랑스어는 수 세기 동안 외교의 국제적 언어였기 때문이다. 만약 불어를 모른다면 이 점에 대해 사전에 사과를 하는 것이 좋다. 그러나 많은 프랑스 비즈니스맨들은 영어를 구사 할 수 있다.

종교

공식적인 종교는 없다. 프랑스는 원래 가톨릭 국가이다.

인구통계

프랑스의 인구는 6천 5백 30만 명이다. 세계 제2차 대전 이후에 도시화가 진행되었으며 이제는 인구의 75%가 도시에 거주하고 있다. 파리에는 9백 79만 명이 거주하고 있다.

비즈니스 관행

약속

- 비즈니스이던 사적인 일이던 항상 약속을 잡아야한다. 시간은 반드시 지키도록 한다. 그러나 프랑스 남부 지방에는 시간 준수에 대해 좀 더 관대하다.
- 대부분 프랑스인들은 여름휴가가 4-5주 정도 된다. 그들은 7월과 8월에 휴가를 많이 간다.
- 프랑스인들 간에는 눈 맞춤을 자주하고 대화를 나누는 사람들 끼리 상대를 계속 쳐다보면서 얘기를 한다.
- 프랑스인들은 위계질서가 매우 엄격하다.
- 여성들은 프랑스 남성들의 기사도 정신을 여성 하대로 오해해서는 안된다.
- 대화를 시작할 때 사적인 질문으로 시작하지 않는다.
- 목소리가 높고 몸짓이 흥분되어 보인다고 해서 반드시 화를 낸다고 생각하면 안된다. 그저 대화 소재에 대해 많은 관심을 갖고 있다는 표현일 뿐이다.
- 프랑스인들은 편지 작성 시 형식을 매우 중요시한다.

비즈니스 접대

- 비즈니스는 중식이나 석식에서도 이루어지지만 점심 식사를 하면서 업무를 하는 것이 가장 바람직하다.
- 점심 식사는 약 2시간 정도 걸릴수도 있다. 저녁 식사는 늦게 이루어진다(대개 오후8시에서 9시에 시작한다.)
- 식사나 음료를 하자고 초대하는 사람이 식대를 내는 것이 원칙이다
- 대부분의 식당들은 예약을 해야 한다.
- 프랑스인들은 입담이 좋은 사람들을 매우 좋아한다.
- 식사시에는 두 손을 항상 테이블 위에 올려놓도록 한다.

- 식사시에는 와인을 곁들이는 것이 일반적이다. 만약 와인을 원하지 않으면 식사 시작전에 와인 전을 거꾸로 엎어 놓으면 된다.
- 사람들의 프라이버시를 존중해야 한다. 프랑스인들은 항상 문을 닫는 습관이 있다. 그들처럼 항상 문을 닫도록 한다. 또한 문을 열어야 할 경우에는 노크를 하고 잠시 기다렸다 들어가도록 한다.

의전

인사

- 사람을 소개 받거나 만났을 때 그리고 헤어질 때 반드시 악수를 한다.
- 사교 모임에서는 두 사람끼리 볼을 맞비비고 입으로 키스 소리를 내는 것은 흔한 일이다.

몸 동작

- 공공장소에서는 껌을 씹지 않는다.
- 손님이나 손윗사람이 들어오면 남성들은 일어서거나 일어서는 시늉이라도 해야 한다.

복장

- 프랑스인들은 복장에 매우 신경을 쓴다. 짙은 색의 정장을 입는 것이 좋다.
- 선물을 줄 때에는 상당한 안목이 있어야 한다.
- 책이나 음악 등은 지적인 관심을 나타내기 때문에 좋은 선물로 간주된다.

일본

역사

일본은 4세기경 야마토 정권이 출현하여 점차 통일 국가를 형성해나갔다. 6세기경에는 쇼토쿠 태자가 수와 신라로부터 선진문화 및 문물제도를 수용해 천황중심적인 집권국가로의 이행을 시도했다. 야마토 정권은 654년 다이카 개신을 일으켜 당의 율령체제를 모방한 국왕중심의 중앙집권체제를 확립하였다. 8세기 말 귀족간의 싸움으로 율령체제가 해이해지자 무사단을 거느린 호족들이 토지를 겸병하는 장원화가 진행됐으며, 12세기 중엽에는 가마쿠라 막부의 무인정치시대가 열렸다. 가마쿠라 막부는 천황으로부터 쇼군의 칭호를 부여받은 무사의 우두머리가 전국을 실질적으로 통치했으며 봉건제도와 유사한 주종관계를 형성했다. 1592년 패권을 잡은 도요토미 히데요시는 임진왜란을 일으키고 도요토미 히데요시가 죽자 도쿠가와 이예야스가 실권을 잡았다. 13세기 후반에는 원의 침입을 막아내는 과정에서 도쿠가와 막부가 점차 쇠퇴되었고 결국 무로마치 막부로 교체되었다. 일본의 막부는 1854년 3월 미일 화친조약을 맺고 1856년 총영사로 부임한 해리스의 사용에 따라 1858년 6월 미일 수호통상조약을 맺었다. 1868년 3월에는 메이지천황이 신정부의 정부 조직을 정비하고, 연호를 메이지로 정하였다. 1869년 신정부를 중앙집권화로 추진하고 근대국가로 발전하게 하는 메이지 유신을 감행했다. 1894년 조선을 둘러싸고 청과 전쟁을 일으켜 승리하게 되고 1895년 청일강화조약을 체결하여 청으로부터 요동반도와 대만 등을 할양받고 배상금을 지불받았다.

러일전쟁 후 일본은 미국, 영국의 승인 하에 한국에 통감부를 두고 외교, 내정, 군사의 실권을 계속 빼앗아 갔다. 급기야 1910년 한국을 병합하여 조선총독부를 두고 식민 지배를 시작했다.

제1차 세계대전 이후 대공황을 겪으면서 일본에서는 우익세력과 군부가 전면에 등장했다. 또한 만

주침략을 계기로 국제사회에서도 고립되어 파시즘적 군국주의로 치달았다. 결국 제 2차 세계대전에서 태평양 전쟁을 일으키고 미국에 의한 원자폭탄 투하로 패배함으로써 군국주의에 종지부를 찍게 되었다. 이후 미국 군정 아래 외부로부터 주어진 민주주의가 시작되고 경제적으로도 회복되기에 이르렀다. 현재 일본은 전쟁이 안겨준 상처를 되새기며 입헌군주제라는 정치체제 아래 아시아의 중심적인 역할을 담당하고 있다.

언어

일본의 공식적 언어는 일어이다. 이는 매우 복잡하고 미묘한 언어이며 세계 어느 곳에서도 모국어로 사용되는 나라가 없다. 일어는 네 단계의 경어로 표현된다. 일본에서의 커뮤니케이션은 상당히 미묘한 부분이 많다. 즉, 문장을 끝까지 완성하지 않아도 상대방이 충분이 알아듣는 경우가 많다.

종교

일본은 전통적인 일본 고유의 종교인 신도교를 갖고 있다. 황제 추대는 신도주의에 의해 지지된다. 그러나 일본인들은 종교적 차이를 존중하며 불교와 신도를 동시에 병행하고 있는 경우도 많다.

인구

일본 현재 인구는 1억 2천 7백만 명이다. 이런 높은 인구밀도는 일본들의 "집단 의식"을 설명하는 요인이된다. 국토의 면적은 지구 총면적의 0.3%이나 인구는 세계 총인구의 3%를 구성하고 있다. 이런 환경 하에서는 순응주의와 단체활동이 갈등을 방지하는 가장 좋은 방법으로 인식되고 있다.

비즈니스 관행

약속

- 항상 시간을 엄수해야한다.
- 일본인이 "고려해 보겠다"는 말을 하면 이는 사실상 "No"라는 의미이다.
- "인맥"은 일본에서 비즈니스를 수행하는데 매우 유익하다.

- 연령은 곧 직위와 같기 때문에 비즈니스를 하는 일본인 중 연장자에게 가상 정중하게 예의를 갖추도록 해야한다.
- 일본인들은 비즈니스 상대에게 그들이 무엇을 기대하는지 정확하게 설명하지 않는다.
- 일본인에게 섣불리 말하거나 거절을 직접접으로 하는 것을 삼간다. 항상 간접적인 표현을 사용해야한다.
- 일본인들은 업무에 대해 매우 진지하다. 분위기를 좀 가볍게 하기 위해 농담을 하는 것은 드문일이다.

비즈니스 접대

- 비즈니스 접대는 업무 시간 이후에 이루어지는 경우가 많으며 가정으로 초대 하는 경우는 매우 드물다.
- 초대를 받게되면 초대하는 측에서 대접을 한다.
- 만약 일본인의 가정으로 초대를 받는다면 이는 대단한 호의임을 명심하고 따라서 감사의 표시를 충분히 해야 한다.
- 식사 중에 젓가락으로 사람을 가리켜서는 안된다. 젓가락을 사용하지 않을 경우에는 젓가락 받침 위에 가지런히 올려놓는 것이 예의이다.
- 식사시 차가 더 필요해서 리필을 받는 경우 반드시 양손으로 들어서 받거나 건네주어야 한다.
- 시간이 경과하면 상대방을 초대하고 싶은 마음이 생기게 된다. 외국인이 돈을 지불하는 것을 한 사코 거절해도 자신이 내겠다고 계속 말해야한다. 일본인을 식사 초대할 경우에는 초대하는 사람이 미국인인 경우에는 양식당으로 초대하는 것이 좋다. 그리고 한국인이라면 한식당으로 초대하는 것이 더욱 좋을 것이다.

의전

인사

- 일본인들은 서양 습관에 대해 매우 민감하다. 따라서 인사로 악수를 청하는 경우가 종종 있다.
- 일본의 전통 인사는 목례이다.

몸 동작

● 팔이나 손을 과다하게 움직이는 몸짓이나 색다른 얼굴 표정 또는 극적인 몸짓은 어떤 경우라도 삼간다.

● 손가락으로 사람이나 사물을 가리키는 것은 무례한 행위로 간주된다.

● 일본인들은 공공장소에서 이성간에 신체를 만지는 것을 탐탁지 않게 여긴다.

● 일본 남성들은 어깨를 두드리는 것이나 상대방의 신체를 만지는 행위를 선호하지 않는다.

● 대화를 할 때 서양 사람들과 대화를 나눌 때보다 조금 더 떨어져서 얘기를 한다.

● 상대를 직접 쳐다보고 눈을 맞추는 것은 피해야한다.

● 일본인들은 침묵을 불편하게 생각하지 않는다. 오히려 유용할 때도 있다.

복장

● 남성들은 정장을 착용하고 캐주얼하게 보여서는 안된다.

● 여성들은 정장을 착용하고 보석이나 향수, 화장을 지나치지 않게 한다.

● 일본은 여름에 매우 덥기 때문에 면 옷을 준비해야한다. 일본인들은 청결에 대해 매우 신경을 쓰기 때문에 갈아입을 옷을 적절하게 준비하도록 한다.

● 일본 전통 의상인 기모노를 입을 경우 항상 왼쪽이 오른쪽을 덮도록 입는다. 오른쪽으로 왼쪽을 덮는 것은 시신에 수의를 입힐 때만 해당된다.

선물

● 선물 증정은 일본에서 매우 흔한 일이다.

● 일본인들에게는 교환되는 선물의 내용 자체 보다 교환의 의식이 더 중요하다.

● 일본인들은 선물을 받는 즉시 열어보지 않는다.

● 선물은 반드시 일본에서 포장을 하거나 호텔이나 꽃집의 포장 서비스를 이용하도록 한다.

● 꽃다발에 짝수의 꽃을 주는 것과 같은 짝수로 선물은 주지 않는다. 4는 죽음과 관련된 숫자이므로 어떤 경우에도 피해야한다.

필리핀

역사

필리핀의 역사는 보르네오 출신인 다투족이 피나이섬으로 상륙했던 13세기부터 시작된다. 필리핀에 최초로 사람이 거주하기 시작한 시기는 30만 년 전이며, 현 조상은 2만 5천년 전 아시아 본토로부터 이주해온 것으로 추정된다.

1521년 스페인의 페르난두 마젤란에 의해 필리핀이 발견되었으며 뒤이어 16세기 말엽 민다나오 섬 지역을 중심으로 이슬람교가 소개되었다. 이 무렵 필리핀 북부와 중부 전 지역이 무력으로 스페인 식민지가 되면서 모든 주민들은 명목상 로마 가톨릭으로 개종했다. 마닐라의 중앙정부는 19세기까지도 중세적 · 독재적 경향을 지니고 있었다. 19세기말 유럽 유학중 민족주의 사상에 고무된 필리핀의 부유한 지주층의 자녀들이 귀국하여 1896년에 폭동사건을 일으켰으나 스페인 군대에 의해 진압되었다.

1898년 미국-스페인 전쟁 뒤 필리핀 제도는 미국에 할양되었으나 필리핀 내 독립운동은 1906년까지 수그러들지 않았다. 1935년 정치적 · 경제적 독립을 꾀하기 위해 필리핀 연방이 수립되었지만 이러한 노력은 제2차 세계대전과 뒤이은 일본의 침략과 점령 때문에 지연되었다.

필리핀은 1944~1945년 미군에 의해 해방을 맞이한 후, 1946년 7월 4일 미국 정부를 본뜬 정부를 세우고 필리핀 공화국 수립을 선포했다. 초대 대통령으로는 마누엘 로하스가 선출되었고 1965년 페르디난드 E. 마르코스가 대통령에 선출되었다. 그러나 마르코스의 오랜 독재와 명백한 부정선거는 폭동을 야기 시켰고, 이 폭동으로 마르코스는 권좌에서 물러나게 되었다. 마르코스 축출 직후인 1986년 2월 25일 코라손 아키노가 대통령에 취임했다. 1992년 5월 마르코스 정부 전복에 견인차 역할을 했던 피델 라모스 국방장관이 아키노의 지지에 힘입어 대통령에 당선되었다. 그러나 필리핀은 현재도 정치와 경제적으로 많은 문제를 겪고 있으며 해결책을 모색하고 있다.

종교

약 83%의 필리핀인은 스스로 가톨릭이라고 하지만 무속 신앙도 상당수 있다.

인구통계

오늘날 1억 7백만 명이 살고 있다. 수도이면서 가장 큰 도시인 마닐라의 인구는 약 1천 348만 명이다.

비즈니스 관행

약속

- 필리핀인들은 외국인들이 비즈니스 약속을 반드시 지켜야한다고 생각한다. 필리핀인들도 비즈니스 미팅에 시간을 맞추어 참석한다.
- 대부분의 경우 필리핀 사교 모임은 약속된 시간 보다 늦게 시작하는 경향이 있다. 그러므로 정시에 도착하는 것은 결례가 될 수 있다. 중요한 손님일수록 늦게 도착하는 것이 예의이다. 도착 시간은 15분에서 약 2 시간 까지 늦어질 수 있다.
- 필리핀에서는 비즈니스 또는 관공서의 모든 비즈니스 거래는 영어로 이루어진다.

비즈니스 접대

- 서양 사람들이 보기에 부적절한 경우에도 필리핀인들이 미소를 짓거나 웃는 경우가 있다. 이는 필리핀인들이 당황스러운 일이나 불화를 숨기기 위한 것이다. 필리핀 의사는 환자에게 병이 깊다는 얘기를 하면서도 미소를 지을 수도 있다.
- 필리핀인들은 모든 사람들은 존중 받을 가치가 있다고 생각한다.
- 조용하고 부드러운 어조로 말해야한다. 필리핀인들은 조화를 중요시 여긴다.
- 필리핀인들과 가까워지면 그들은 매우 사교적이고 대화를 쉽게 나눈다는 것을 알게 된다.
- 음식은 필리핀 문화에서 매우 중요하다. 사교모임에는 항상 음식이 있다.

의전

인사

● 외국 비즈니스맨들은 필리핀인에게 소개를 받거나 추후 다시 만나게 되면 악수를 해야 한다.

● 필리핀에서는 전통적으로 공공장소에서 이성간의 신체 접촉은 없었다.

● 필리핀 여성 간에는 만났을 때 포옹과 볼에 키스 하는 경우가 자주 있다.

몸 동작

● 손가락으로 사람이나 사물을 가리키는 것은 모욕적인 몸동작이다.

● 필리핀에서는 사람을 오래 동안 쳐다보는 것은 부정적 의미가 크다.

● 양손을 허리에 얹은채 서 있는 것은 바람직하지 않다. 이는 사람들에게 항상 호전적인 자세로 받아들여진다.

복장

● 필리핀은 덥고 습하기 때문에 필리핀 비즈니스 복장은 대체로 캐주얼하다. 남성들은 짙은 색 바지와 흰색 반팔 셔츠를, 여성들은 짙은 색 치마와 흰색 긴팔 블라우스를 입는다.

● 외국인인 경우 만나는 사람들에 따라 어떤 복장이 요구되는지 파악할 때 까지는 수수한 복장을 유지하는 것이 좋다.

● 필리핀 남성들은 바롱 타가롱 (barong tagalong)이라는 자수 놓은 셔츠를 입기도 한다.

● 남성과 여성 모두는 해변에 있는 경우를 제외하고는 공공장소에서 반바지를 입거나 샌들을 신으면 안된다.

선물

● 선물을 주는 것은 필리핀 사회에서 매우 중요한 일이다. 가장 흔한 선물은 꽃이나 음식이다.

● 필리핀 가정에 초대를 받으면 안주인에게 꽃, 캔디 또는 초콜릿을 선물하는 것이 좋다.

싱가포르

역사

19세기에 들어설 때까지는 작은 어촌에 지나지 않던 싱가포르가 역사에 등장한 것은 1819년 영국인 토머스 스탬퍼드 래플즈가 싱가포르강 하구에 상륙하여 개발에 착수하면서 부터였다. 1824년 싱가포르에 동인도 회사를 설립하여 동서의 중계 무역자로서 급속히 발전하였고 이로 인해 국제항의 기반이 이루어졌다.

그 후 1832년 영국의 해협식민지의 중심이 되고, 1870년대의 수에즈 운하 개통과 함께 더욱 중요한 위치를 차지하게 되었다. 제2차 세계대전 중인 1942년 2월 15일부터 3년 8개월 동안 일본군에 점령되어 소남시라고 개명 되었다. 싱가포르 함락 때 일어난 싱가포르 학살 사건은 그 희생자가 3만 명이나 된다.

제 2차 세계대전 후 다시 영국의 식민지가 되었고, 1957년에 말레이시아 연방으로 독립했다. 1959년 리 쾅 유씨를 초대 수상으로 한 말레이시아 자치주의 지위를 얻었다. 1965년 말레이시아 연방의 말레이시아인 우대정책과 리 쾅 유씨를 당수로 하는 인민행동당의 인종 간 평등주의에서 심각하게 대립하게 되었고, 그로 인해 말레이시아 연방의 라만 정권은 싱가포르의 분리를 결정했다. 1965년 8월 9일, 싱가포르는 말레이시아로부터 완전히 독립하여 대통령을 원수로 하는 완전한 독립주권국가가 되었다.

독립 후 리 수상의 지도 아래 눈부신 발전을 이루어, 현재는 아시아의 신흥 경제 국가로 부상하여 주목되고 있다.

언어

싱가포르에는 네 개의 공식 언어가 있다 ; 말레이어, 타밀, 중국어 그리고 영어이다. 싱가포르의 삼분 화된 인종적 집단을 통일하기 위해 싱가포르에서는 교육, 비즈니스 그리고 정부 기관에서는 영어를 사용한다.

인구통계

도시국가인 싱가포르에는 579만 명이 살고 있다. 번창한 무역 중심지인 싱가포르는 다양한 인종들이 모여 살고 있다. 싱가포르인의 대부분은 중국인이다.

종교

원주민 말레이의 대부분은 회교이지만 모든 회교도들이 반드시 말레이는 아니다. 회교도들은 총 인 구의 15%에 달한다. 이와 마찬가지로 기독교 역시 여러 다른 인종적 집단에서 믿는 종교이다. 싱가포 르 사람의 대부분은 중국인이다.

비즈니스 관행

약속

- 모든 비즈니스 약속 시간은 반드시 엄수해야 한다.
- 대부분의 비즈니스 거래에 사용되는 언어는 영어이다.
- 싱가포르 예절에서는 반대 의견을 직접 드러내지 않게 되어있으므로 "No"라는 말은 자주 들을 수 가 없다. 예의 바르지만 분명하지 않은 "Yes"는 상대방에게 불쾌감을 주지 않으려는 테크닉이다. 싱가포르에서 "Yes"는 "동의합니다"에서부터 "글쎄" 그리고 "제 무관심한 태도로 보아 사실은 No 라고 하는 것을 이해하기 바랍니다." 까지 다양하게 해석될 수 있다.
- 싱가포르에서 성공적인 관계를 갖는 데에 있어 가장 중요한 요소는 공손함이다.
- 싱가포르 사람들은 서양인의 입장에서 보기에는 적절하지 않는 상황에서 미소를 짓거나 웃을 수 있다.

- 싱가포르에서는 사람들 앞에 드러내 놓고 화를 내는 것은 부끄러운 일이다. 이런 사람은 신뢰나 존경을 받을 수 없다.
- 조용하고 부드러운 어조로 말해야한다. 항상 평정을 유지하도록 한다. 내가 한 말에 상대방이 대답할 수 있는 시간을 충분히 주어야 한다.
- 좋은 대화 소재는 관광, 여행, 미래 계획 그리고 조직에서의 성공에 관한 것들이다.

비즈니스 접대

- 음식은 싱가포르 문화에서 매우 중요하다. 사교 모임에는 항상 음식이 포함된다.
- 사교 모임에 초대 받으면 반드시 참석하는 것이 좋다. 성공적인 비즈니스 관계를 구축하려면 좋은 사회적 관계를 구축하는 것 여하에 달려 있다.
- 싱가포르의 반 부정부패법은 매우 엄격하기 때문에 공무원들은 사교 모임 참석이 금지되어 있는 경우도 있다.

의전

인사

- 싱가포르는 중국, 말레이 그리고 인도의 세 개의 주요 인종 집단이 있으며 이들은 각각의 전통을 갖고 있다.
- 젊거나 외국에서 수학한 싱가포르인들과 인사할 경우 악수가 가장 흔한 인사 방법이다.
- 싱가포르에서 서구화된 여성들은 남성, 여성 모두와 악수를 한다.
- 전통적인 말레이 인사는 'salaam'이라고 하며 이는 악수는 하되 손을 잡지 않는 악수의 유형이다. 쌍방은 각각 한쪽 손을 펴서 내밀어 상대가 내미는 손에 살짝 대었다가 그 손을 가슴 위에 얹는다.
- 대부분의 싱가포르 인디언은 힌두 신자이다. 그들은 이성간의 접촉을 금하고 있다. 남성이나 여성 모두 동성 간에만 악수를 한다. 그러나 서구화된 힌두들은 이성과도 악수를 한다. 전통적인 인도 인사는 손을 합장하고 살짝 목례를 하는 것이다.

몸 동작

- 싱가포르에서는 악수를 제외하고는 이성간에는 공공연한 신체 접촉은 하지 않는다. 공공장소에서 이성을 키스하거나 포옹하면 안된다.
- 회교와 힌두 모두에 있어 왼손은 부정한 손으로 간주한다. 식사 시에는 반드시 오른손을 사용한다. 왼손으로 물건이나 사람을 만져서는 안된다.
- 발도 부정한 것으로 간주한다. 발로 물건을 치우면 안 되며 발로 물건을 만져서도 안된다.
- 집게 손가락으로 사람을 가리켜서는 안된다. 말레이들은 동물을 가리킬 때만 집게손을 이용한다.
- 대부분의 인디언이나 말레이들은 머리가 영혼이 있는 곳으로 생각한다. 사람들의 머리를 절대로 만지면 안 되며 어린 아이의 머리를 쓰다듬는 것도 이에 포함된다.

복장

- 싱가포르는 적도에서 북위 136.8km에 있다. 그러므로 일 년 내내 덥고 습하다. 기온은 섭씨 24-31도이며 습도는 90%를 상회한다.
- 이런 높은 기온과 습도로 인해 싱가포르 비즈니스 복장은 캐주얼한 경우가 많다.

선물

- 싱가포르는 아시아에서 가장 청렴한 국가라는 점을 자랑스럽게 생각하고 있다.
- 중국인들은 선물을 받기 전에 세 번 거절하는 것이 전통이다. 이는 그들이 욕심꾸러기로 보이지 않게 하기 위한 것이다. 그러나 받을 때 까지 권해야한다. 선물을 드디어 받으면 선물을 받아주어 고맙다고 인사해야한다.

대만

역사

타이완의 역사는 230년 중국이 타이완을 최초로 경영하였다는 기록에서 시작된다. 당나라 이후 송나라 때까지는 많은 사람들이 중국 연해에서 타이완으로 이주하였다. 원나라 초기에는 중국의 적극적인 해외진출로 인해 1360년 펑후에 순검사가 설치되었고 중국의 푸젠성 둥안현에 예속되었다.

1622년에 네덜란드가 펑후를, 1624년 남부 타이완을 점령한 데 이어 1626년 스페인이 지룽·단수이를 점거하였다가 1642년 철수하였다. 1661년 명나라의 정성공이 네덜란드를 철수시키고 타이완 개척의 기틀을 마련하기 시작하였다. 18세기 후반부터는 이주민이 급증하여 개척이 빠르게 진행되고 행정구역도 확대되었다.

중국과 영국의 아편전쟁 후 1858년 톈진조약에 따라 타이완 북부의 단수이가 유럽 열강의 각축장이 되었다. 1894~1895년간 청·일 전쟁은 타이완을 일본에게 51년간 식민 지배를 받게 하였다.

1884년 프랑스함대가 펑후를 점령하여 이듬해 청·프 전쟁이 일어났고, 타이완성으로 개칭되었다. 1895년 일본은 초대 타이완총독에 하바야마 모토기 해군대장을 임명하고 이듬해 군정을 폐지하였으며 타이완총독에 입법권을 위임하는 <법률 제63호>를 공포하였다.

1897년 시모노세키조약에 따라 일본은 타이완 근대화를 위한 개혁을 실시하였으나 정치적 차별정책으로 반일 감정이 격화되어 1895년 타이완민주국 건설, 1920년 타이완의회 설치 청원운동 등의 항일운동이 전개되었다. 1945년 7월 일본이 패전함으로써 타이완은 중국에 반환되었다.

1949년 중국 본토에서 중화인민공화국이 성립함에 따라 장제스는 국민당정부를 타이완으로 옮기고 대륙수복의 기치 아래 경제발전을 통한 국력신장에 주력하였다. 정책적으로는 불접촉·불담판·

불간섭의 3불정책을 고수하면서 본토와의 대하에 응하지 않다가 1987년 7월, 38년 만에 민간인의 중국거주 친척방문을 허용하였다.

1990년대에 이르러서는 중국과 타이완 사이에 제한된 무역중계망이 설치되었고 현재는 중국과 공식적, 비공식적으로 교류를 확대해나가고 있다.

언어

대만의 공식 언어는 전통 만다린 중국어이다. 그러나 대만어가 더 많이 사용되고 있다. 대만인들은 현재 중화인민공화국에서 사용하는 간자를 사용하지 않는다. 영어는 학교에서 매우 인기 있는 과목이며 대부분의 비즈니스인들은 영어를 구사하고 알아들으며 서류도 영어로 작성한다.

종교

종교적 분포는 불교, 유교, 도교 합이 93%, 기독교 4.5%, 그리고 기타 종교가 2.5%이다.

인구통계

대만 인구는 약 2천 3백 70만 명이며 주로 대만인과 본토 중국인으로 구성되어 있다. 대만의 원주민은 인구의 2%에 불과하다. 대만 인구의 55%는 30세 이하이다.

비즈니스 관행

약속

- 약속 시간은 항상 지켜야한다. 이는 외국인에게도 요구되며 예의가 바르다는 표시이다.
- 대만 교통은 매우 혼잡하다. 약속 장소가 가까워서 걸어갈 수 있는 경우를 제외하고는 사전에 일찍 출발하는 것이 좋다.

비즈니스 접대

- 대만에서는 손님을 후하게 대접하는 것을 매우 중요하게 생각한다. 업무 시간 후에 여러 차례 식사 초대를 받게 될 것이다.
- 사전에 약속하지 않고 남의 집을 방문하면 안된다.
- 좋은 대화 소재는 중국 관광명소, 예술, 서예, 가족 그리고 상대방 가족의 건강에 대한 것들이다.

의전

인사

- 사람을 처음 소개받을 경우 목례를 하는 것으로 충분하다.
- 친구나 지인을 만나면 악수를 하는 것이 적절하다. 양팔을 몸에 붙이고 다리를 모은 후 목례를 하면 예의가 바른 인사가 된다.
- 대만에서는 연장자들을 상당히 존중하기 때문에 항상 그들과 먼저 얘기를 나누는 것이 예의바른 것이다.
- 식사 했냐는 질문을 받아도 놀랄 필요가 없다. 이는 봉건시대 기근을 거친 과정에서 파생된 매우 흔한 인사이다. 이는 서양에서 "How are you?"와 같은 인사로 생각하면 된다. 혹 식사를 안했더라도 "Yes"라고 하는 것이 예의바른 대답이다.
- 모임이나 파티에서는 다른 사람들에게 소개 받을 때 까지 기다린다.

몸 동작

- 친근감의 표시로라도 다른 사람에게 윙크를 하면 안된다.
- 다른 사람의 어깨를 팔로 감싸면 안된다.
- 다른 사람들의 어린 아이 머리를 만져서는 안된다. 어린이들은 소중하게 여겨지며 부주의하게 다루면 다칠 수 있다고 생각한다.
- 중국인들은 손을 펴서 사물이나 사람을 가리킨다. 손가락을 사용하는 것은 무례하다고 생각한다.

복장

● 캐주얼한 활동에는 검소한 옷차림을 한다.

선물

● 선물을 주거나 받을 경우 반드시 두 손을 사용한다. 받은 선물은 준 사람 앞에서 열어보지 않는다.

● 중국인들은 다음의 물건을 죽음과 연관 짓는다. 그러므로 다음의 것들은 선물로 주는 것을 삼간다 ;

   – 짚으로 만든 샌들

   – 시계

   – 황새나 두루미

   – 손수건

   – 선물이나 포장지의 주된 색깔이 희색, 검정색 또는 푸른색

● 칼이나 가위 또는 절단용 도구를 주는 것도 피해야한다. 중국인들에게 이런 물건들은 절교를 의미한다.

미합중국

역사

미국의 역사는 유럽인의 이주와 함께 시작되었으며 유럽인의 이주가 시작 된 것은 콜럼버스의 항해로 부터 긴 세월이 지난 17세기 이후였다.

영국이 미국으로 이주한 유럽인에게 과중한 세금을 부과하고 가혹한 통치를 하자, 미국의 13개 주가 단결하여 독립 전쟁을 일으켰으며, 이듬해인 1776년 마침내 독립군인 아메리카 합중국이 탄생했다.

독립 당시 13개의 주의 약 400만 인구로 출발한 미국은 원주민인 인디언들의 강력한 저항을 물리치며 서부를 개척해 나아가, 19세기 중반 태평양 연안까지 이르게 되었다.

1848년 34개 주로 국토가 넓어지자, 상공업을 중심으로 하는 북부 지역과 농업을 중심으로 하는 남부 지역 간에 대립이 생겨 4년에 걸친 남북전쟁이 발발하게 되었다. 전쟁의 결과 자유와 평등을 주장하는 북부가 흑인 노예 제도를 유지시켜야 한다는 남부에 승리하여 남북통일을 이루게 되었다.

한편, 제1차 세계대전 당시 먼로 독트린 이래 고립 정책을 고수하던 미국은 미국의 선박들이 독일의 U보트에 의해 계속 파괴되자 이에 분개하여 제1차 세계대전에 참전한다. 제1차 세계대전 동안 전쟁 물자를 팔아 수입을 올렸던 미국은 전쟁이 끝나 물품에 대한 수요가 없게 되자 1929년 전 세계를 혼란에 빠뜨리는 대공황을 겪게 된다.

그러나 1939년 9월 1일 독일이 일으킨 제2차 세계대전에 연합국의 자격으로 참전, 전쟁을 승리로 이끌어 미국은 크게 부상하게 된다.

제2차 세계대전 이후 미국은 사회주의 진영과 자본주의 진영 간의 냉전과 흑인 인권운동이라는 역

사적 전환점을 통해 국제적으로 강력한 힘을 발휘하고 있으며 오늘날까지 세계 최강국으로서의 면모를 지키고 있다.

언어

영어는 미국의 공식 언어이다. 스페인어는 가장 널리 사용되는 제2외국어이다.

종교

미국에서는 종교와 국가는 항상 별개의 것으로 간주되었다. 그러나 미국 시민들의 75%는 종교를 갖고 있다. 대부분은 기독교이다. 유태교와 이슬람교는 인구의 2%에 이른다.

인구통계

미합중국의 인구는 약 3억 3천만 명이다. 가장 큰 도시는 뉴욕이며 뉴욕 내에만 약 8백 20만 명이 그리고 그 주변에는 더 많은 사람들이 거주하고 있다.

비즈니스 관행

약속

- 시간 엄수는 매우 중요하다. 초대를 받았을 경우 시간에 맞추어 도착해야한다.
- 미국인들은 날짜를 쓸 때 월, 일, 연도의 순으로 작성한다. 예를 들면 2007년 12월 3일은 12/3/07 과 같이 쓴다.
- 사전 약속은 반드시 해야 한다.
- 편의점들은 대개 24시간 영업한다.

비즈니스 접대

- 외식을 할 경우 친구들 간에 식대를 나누는 경우도 있다. 이는 "splitting the bill", "getting separate checks" 또는 "going Dutch"라고 표현하기도 한다.

- 친구를 방문하기 전에는 전화를 해야 한다.
- 파티 주빈이 초대할 때 사전에 복장에 대해 얘기를 해주는 경우를 제외하고는 대부분의 파티는 캐주얼 차림이다.
- 음식이나 음료를 권했다고 해서 반드시 먹거나 마셔야 하는 것은 아니다. 또한 주빈이 음식을 먹으라고 계속 권하지 않을 테니 먹고 싶을 때 스스로 알아서 먹으면 된다.
- 미국인들은 음식을 손으로 먹는 경우가 많다. 다른 사람들이 어떻게 하는지 관찰하고 따른다. 만약 손으로 먹는 것이 편하지 않으면 자신이 편한 방법으로 먹도록 한다.
- 미국에서는 길을 걸으면서 먹는 것은 무례한 행동이 아니다. 많은 사람들은 차에서 그리고 심지어는 운전하면서 음식을 먹기도 한다.

의전

인사
- 일반적인 인사는 스마일이고 목례를 하거나 손을 흔들거나 말로 인사하면 된다.
- 비즈니스 관계에서는 악수를 하는 것이 좋다.
- 일반적으로 동성 친구 간에는 손을 잡지 않는다.
- 등을 두드리는 것은 친근감의 표시이다.
- 작별 인사를 할 때 손을 펴서 흔들며 인사한다.
- 사람의 눈을 직접 맞추는 것은 진지함을 나타낸다. 그러나 정도가 지나치면 안된다. 소수민족 중에는 눈을 돌리는 경우도 있다.
- 다른 사람에게 물건을 건네줄 때 살짝 던져주거나 한 손으로 건네주어도 된다.

복장
- 도시에서는 정장 착용이 가장 좋다.
- 지방이나 소도시에서는 사람들의 복장은 좀 더 캐주얼하고 소박하다.

- 근무 중이 아닌 경우에는 캐주얼한 복장을 하도록 한다.
- 자기 나라 전통 의상을 입고 싶다면 그렇게 해도 된다.

선물

- 비즈니스 거래에서 선물 증정은 법적으로 권장하지 않는다.
- 다른 사람들의 가정을 방문할 시에는 선물을 반드시 가져갈 필요는 없지만 만약 준비한다면 상대 방이 고맙게 여길 것이다. 선물로는 꽃, 화분 또는 와인 같은 것이 좋다.
- 만약 미국인의 가정에 며칠 머물게 될 경우 선물을 주는 것이 적절하다. 또한 감사의 편지를 쓰는 것도 좋다.
- 선물을 주기에 좋은 시기는 도착했을 때 또는 떠날 때이다. 가장 좋은 선물은 본국에서 가져온 것 이다.
- 사람들을 식사 또는 공연에 초대하는 것은 매우 일반적인 선물이다.

Appendix B

Listening Dialogues

Listening 1 (p 6)

Dialogue 1:

Person 1　What do you do?

Person 2　I work for ticketing at an amusement park.

Person 1　Oh really! Do you like it?

Person 2　Yes I do, it's really fun.

Person 1　What are your responsibilities?

Person 2　I greet customers and check their tickets.

Dialogue 2:

Person 1　Where do they work?

Person 2　They work at Royal Hotel.

Person 1　Oh yeah, what do they do?

Person 2　They're waitresses.

Dialogue 3:

Person 1　What does she do?

Person 2　She's a flight attendant for an international airline.

Person 1　Does she like it?

Person 2　Yes, she does.

Listening 2 (p 9)

Person 1	Hello, I'm Susan. What's your name?
Person 2	My name's Amy.

Person 1	Hi Amy, I like your uniform, what do you do?
Person 2	I'm a receptionist. I work for Rain Forest Hotel.

Person 1	Oh really, do you like it?
Person 2	Yes, I do. I get to meet a lot of people.

Person 1	How long have you been working there?
Person 2	I've been working there for about 2 years now.

Person 1	Wow, that's a long time. What are your responsibilities?
Person 2	I answer the phone and take reservations.

Person 1	That sounds like a good job!
Person 2	What do you do?

Person 1	I'm a waitress.
Person 2	Where do you work?

Person 1	I work at a small sandwich restaurant.
Person 2	Do you like it?

Person 1	No, I don't. It's really tiring. I wish I could work in a hotel.

Listening 3 (p 10)

Person 1	What do you do?
Person 2	I'm a travel agent.

Person 1	What are your responsibilities?
Person 2	I plan holidays and make reservations.

Person 1	How long have you been working there?
Person 2	I've been working there for about 3 years.

Person 1	Where do you work?
Person 2	I work in a travel agency called Backpack Travel.

Person 1	Oh really? I know that company. Where are you from?
Person 2	I'm from Korea. What do you do?

Person 1	I'm a waitress.
Person 2	Where do you work?

Person 1	I work in a café called Coffee Breaks.
Person 2	How long have you been working there?

Person 1	I've been working there for about 6 months.

Unit **02**

Listening Scripts

Listening 1 (p 17)

Dialogue 1:

 Customer   Excuse me, can you tell me where I can park my car?

Bellhop   Yes ma'am, there is a parking lot in the basement, The entrance is behind the building.

Customer   Thank you.

Dialogue 2:

Customer   Can you tell me where the fitness center is?

Receptionist   Yes, it is next to the swimming pool on the rooftop.

Customer   Thank you.

Dialogue 3:

Customer   Do you have a phone I can use?

Receptionist   Yes sir, there are pay phones on the second floor next to the business center.

Customer   Thank you.

Dialogue 4:

Customer   Hi, I made a reservation in your hotel restaurant.
Can you tell me where it is?

Receptionist   Yes, it's upstairs on the third floor.

Customer   Great, thank you.

Dialogue 5:

Customer   Hi, I would like to change some money.

Receptionist   We have an exchange bureau on the second floor next to the business center.

Customer   Thank you.

Dialogue 6:

Customer   Can you tell me where the coffee shop is?

Receptionist   Yes, it's here on the first floor in front of the elevators.

Customer   Thank you.

Listening 2 (p 19)

1   Go straight two blocks and turn right. It will be on your left between the restaurant and the bakery.

2   Go two blocks and turn left. It will be on your right.

3   Go one block and turn right. Go one more block and turn left. It will be the first shop on your right. It's across from the post office.

4   Go one block and turn right. Go past the hair salon and it will be on your right. It's across from the car center and next to the hotel.

5   Go straight two blocks and turn right. Go straight to the next intersection and turn left. It will be on your left across from the department store

Unit **03**

Listening Scripts

Listening 1 (p 27)

Dialogue 1:

Receptionist   Can I help you?

Customer   Yes, can you tell me when the next train leaves for Seoul?

Receptionist   Certainly sir, one moment please...
Thank you for waiting, it leaves at a quarter to four this afternoon.

Customer   Thank you.

Dialogue 2:

Customer   Hi, can you tell me when the exchange bureau opens today?

Receptionist   Yes, certainly, it opens every weekday at 9 a.m.

Customer   Uh..okay, thank you.

Dialogue 3:

Receptionist   Good morning, Asia Air, how may I help you?

Customer   Good morning, I'd like to make a reservation for a flight to Japan please.

Receptionist   Certainly ma'am, when would you like to travel?

Customer   On June 4th.

Receptionist   We have one flight leaving at 10:10 a.m. on June 4th, would that be okay?

Customer   That's great, thank you.

Unit 04
Listening Scripts

Listening 1 (p 34)

Dialogue 1:

Waiter	What would you like for dessert, ma'am?
Customer	I'd like the raspberry tart and a coffee.
Waiter	Would you like cream or milk?
Customer	I'd like cream, please.
Waiter	Thank you. May I have your room number?

Dialogue 2:

Customer	What do you recommend?
Waiter	I recommend the grilled steak. It's delicious.
Customer	Okay, I'd like to try the grilled steak.
Waiter	How would you like it done?
Customer	I'd like it medium well done, please.

Dialogue 3:

Waiter   Would you like a baked potato or vegetables?

Woman   I'd like vegetables, please.

Waiter   How would you like them done?

Woman   I'd like them steamed, please.

Waiter   And for you, sir?

Man   I'd like sautéed vegetables, please.

Dialogue 4:

Waiter   What would you like for your entrée?

Customer   Hmm…. What's the salmon with almonds like?

Waiter   It's a grilled, fresh salmon. It's very flavorful.

Customer   And what's the chicken in plum sauce like?

Waiter   It's roasted chicken. It's a little bit sweet.

Customer   Thank you. I'll have the salmon, please.

Please, Come Again

Unit 05 — Listening Scripts

Listening 1 (p 42)

Waiter: Good afternoon. Here is your menu and wine list. The soup of the day is tomato soup. Today's special is grilled salmon with a side salad. I'll be back to take your order when you're ready. Would you care for anything to drink?

Customer: Yes, please. I'll have a coke.

Waiter: Are you ready to order?

Customer: Yes, I am.

Waiter: What would you like to start with?

Customer: I'd like the cheese and bread.

Waiter: And what would you like for the main course?

Customer: I'll have the roasted chicken.

Waiter: What would you like with that?

Customer: What do you have?

Waiter: Side salad, baked potato, or rice.

Customer: I'd like the rice, please

Waiter: Would you like anything else?

Customer: That's all. Thank you.

Unit **06** Listening Scripts

Listening 1 (p 52)

Travel agent	Good afternoon, how may I help you?
Customer	I'd like to make a reservation, please.

Travel agent — Okay, where would you like to go sir?

Customer — I'd like to go to Vancouver.

Travel agent — Okay, great and when would you like to leave?

Customer — I'd like to leave on September 12th.

Travel agent — Okay, when would you like to return?

Customer — I'd like to return on September 24th.

Travel agent — Would you like to fly first class or economy sir?

Customer — First class, please.

Travel agent — One moment please, let me check for you.

Thank you for waiting. I am very sorry sir but we don't have any first class seats available, but there is one economy seat open.

Customer — Okay, thanks fine, I'll take it.

Travel agent — May I have your name please, sir?

Customer — Yes, it's Mr. John Smith.

Travel agent — May I have your passport number Mr. Smith?

Customer — Yes it's ML024132.

Travel agent — Okay sir, the total comes to $745 plus tax.

How would you like to pay?

Customer — Thanks, I'll pay by credit card.

Unit 07

Listening Scripts

Listening 1 (p 58)

1   The restaurant opens for lunch from 11:00 a.m. to 2:30. p.m.

2   What time does the exchange bureau open?

3   Can I get a wake up call for 7:00 a.m.?

4   Where is the coffee shop?

5   Do all the rooms have internet access?

6   Our conference room has seating for 200 people.

7   Please enjoy our complimentary continental breakfast in the morning.

8   Where can I get a city tour?

9   Can you please call me a taxi?

10   How late is room service available?

Unit 08

Listening Scripts

Listening 1 (p 67)

Receptionist	Good afternoon, how may I help you?
Customer	Yes, I'd like to make a reservation please.

Receptionist Certainly, ma'am. May I have your name please?
Customer Yes, it's Ms. Julie MacKay.

Receptionist When will you be arriving Ms. MacKay?
Customer On October 2nd.

Receptionist For how many nights?
Customer For 2 nights. I will check out on the 4th.

Receptionist Okay, and what type of room would you like, Ms. MacKay?
Customer A double room, please.

Receptionist Would you like smoking or non-smoking?
Customer Non-smoking, please.

Receptionist Okay, that comes to a total of $150. How would you like to pay?
Customer I'll pay by credit card. Do you accept Visa?

Receptionist Yes, that's fine. Can I have your card number please?
Customer Yes, it's 4500 6000 3456 4635.

Receptionist And can I have the expiry date, please?
Customer Yes, it's 03/25.

Receptionist Okay Ms. MacKay, I can confirm your reservation. That's a double room for 2 nights from October 2nd. Is this correct?
Customer Yes it is. Thank you.

Receptionist Thank you and we look forward to seeing you on October 2nd.

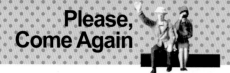

Unit **09**

Listening Scripts

Listening 1 (p 78)

Receptionist Good evening sir, can I help you?

Customer Yes, my name is Jim MacDonald. I have a reservation for a double room for tonight.

Receptionist Okay, let me check Mr. MacDonald... That's a double room for 1 night?

Customer Yes it is.

Receptionist Okay, can you fill out this registration form please?

Customer Sure, here you are.

Receptionist Thank you sir. Here is your key card. Your room is on the sixth floor.

Customer Thank you.

Receptionist Thank you, and I hope you enjoy your stay.

Listening 2 (p 79)

Receptionist	Good morning, sir. May I help you?
Customer	Yes, I would like to check out later today. What's the usual check out time?

Receptionist   It is 11 a.m.

Customer   Okay, can I pay my bill now?

Receptionist   Sure, may I have your room number please?

Customer   Yes it's 1112.

Receptionist   Okay, let me check that for you sir. The total comes to $142.50. How would you like to pay?

Customer   I'll pay by Visa please, here you are.

Receptionist   Thank you and can you sign here, please?

Customer   Certainly.

Receptionist   Okay, thank you sir. Here is your receipt, and I hope you enjoyed your stay with us.

Customer   Thank you.

Please, Come Again

Unit 10

Listening Scripts

Listening 1 (p 86)

🧑 Guide	Korea-Seoul Tours, how can I help you?
🧑 Tourist	I'd like to get some information about day tours of the city.

🧑 Guide	Sure, no problem. There are many tours you can take to see you the sights.
🧑 Tourist	I would like to book a city bus tour for tomorrow.
🧑 Guide	Sure, no problem.

🧑 Tourist	What is included in the tour?
🧑 Guide	The tour includes a restaurant lunch and transportation.

🧑 Tourist	What sites will I see?
🧑 Guide	You'll see the National Gallery, City Park and an ancient temple.

🧑 Tourist	When will the tour leave?
🧑 Guide	The tour bus will leave from your hotel at 9:30 a.m.

🧑 Tourist	And when will the tour return?
🧑 Guide	The tour will return at 6 p.m.

🧑 Tourist	Okay, I'll book two seats, please.
🧑 Guide	Thank you, that will be 60 dollars each, please.

208

Unit **11**

Listening Scripts

Listening 1 (p 94)

Dialogue 1:

Receptionist   Thank you for calling Hotel Vista. How may I help you?

Caller   Yes, I'd like to speak to Mr. Johnson.

Receptionist   I'm sorry, he is in a meeting right now. Can I take a message?

Caller   No thanks, I'll call again later.

Dialogue 2:

Receptionist   Good afternoon. How may I help you?

Caller   Could I speak to the manager, please.

Receptionist   I'm sorry, he is unavailable right now. Can I take a message?

Caller   Yes, please. Could you ask him to call me back, please?

Receptionist   Sure, what's your phone number?

Caller   It's 02-894-7894.

Dialogue 3:

Receptionist Good afternoon. How may I help you?

Caller Could I speak to Miss. Lee, please?

Receptionist I'm sorry, she is out to lunch. Can I take a message?

Caller Yes. I would like to change my reservation from September 20th to September 21st.

Dialogue 4:

Receptionist Hello. How may I help you?

Caller Yes, could I speak to your manager, please?

Receptionist I'm sorry, she is unavailable. Can I take a message?

Caller Yes, please ask her to call me back. It's very important!

Listening 2 (p 95)

Dialogue 1:

Receptionist   Hello, thank you for calling A-List Hotel. My name is Gina, how may I help you?

Mr. Lee   Yes, I would like to speak to the manager, Mr. Kim.

Receptionist   I'm sorry. Mr. Kim is in a meeting right now. Would you like to leave a message?

Mr. Lee   Yes, I would like to change my reservation. I would like to change from March 13th to March 26th. It's very urgent!

Receptionist   Would you like Mr. Kim to call you back?

Mr. Lee   Yes, please. My number is 010-1234-6789.

Receptionist   When is the best time for him to return your call?

Mr. Lee   Please ask him call me before 5 p.m.

Receptionist   May I ask who's calling, please?

Mr. Lee   It's Mr. Lee from Canada-Korea Tour Company

Receptionist   Okay, just to confirm, you would like to change your reservation from March 13th to March 26th?

Mr. Lee   Yes, thank you.

Dialogue 2:

Receptionist   Hello, thank you for calling Seoul City Tours. How can I help you?

Mrs. Jones   I would like to speak to my tour guide, Mr. Park.

Receptionist   May I ask who's calling?

Mrs. Jones   This is Mrs. Jones.

Receptionist   Mr. Park is on a tour right now, can I take a message?

Mrs. Jones   Yes, I need to know how much my tour will cost.

Receptionist   Okay, you need to know the price? Should I have Mr. Park call you back?

Mrs. Jones   No, I am calling long distance from Canada. I will call again at 4 p.m.

Receptionist   Okay, I will give him the message. Thank you

Unit **12**

Listening Scripts

Listening 1 (p 104)

Check-in Clerk	Good afternoon. May I see your ticket and passport please?
Passenger	Yes, here you are.
Check-in Clerk	Would you like a window or an aisle seat?
Passenger	I would like an aisle seat please.
Check-in Clerk	How many bags do you have to check-in?
Passenger	One suitcase.
Check-in Clerk	Could you please place your bag on the scale?
Passenger	Sure.
Check-in Clerk	Okay, that's 20 kilograms. Do you have any carry-on bags?
Passenger	Yes, I have one.
Check-in Clerk	Okay, your boarding time is 6:20 p.m. Please go through security one hour before boarding.
Passenger	And what is the gate number?
Check-in Clerk	You're boarding from gate 32C.
Passenger	Thank you.
Check-in Clerk	Enjoy your flight!

Unit **13**

Listening Scripts

Listening 1 (p 112)

| Officer | Good afternoon, ma'am. How may I help you? |
| Customer | Yes, I'd like to change some money please. |

| Officer | Sure, how much would you like to change? |
| Customer | I'd like to change 1,000,000 yen into US dollars, please. |

| Officer | We charge a 3% commission. Is that okay? |
| Customer | Yes, that's fine. |

| Officer | Okay, that comes to 912 dollars and 30 cents, US. |
| Customer | Thank you. |

| Officer | Thank you, have a nice day. |

Unit **14** Listening Scripts

Listening 1 (p 118)

Employee	Hi, welcome to Happy Valley. Can I see your ticket?
Customer	Sure, here you are. How much is the Tiger Show?

Employee   It's included in the day pass.

Customer   Really, that's great! What time does it start?

Employee   It starts at 10 a.m., then it's on the hour every hour until 9 p.m.

Customer   How long is the show?

Employee   It's 30 minutes.

Customer   And where is it?

Employee   It's in Africa Land. Here, I'll give you an English Park Guide.

Customer   Thank you.

Employee   Thank you, enjoy your day!

참 고 문 헌

김성건(1997), 「싱가포르 사회와 문화」, 문경출판사.

김인호(1997), 「백과사전 세계지리 · 세계사」, 금성출판사

동서역사문화연구회(2007), 「교양세계사」, 우물이 있는 집.

미야자키 마사카츠(2008), 「하룻밤에 읽는 세계사」, 랜덤하우스

안병직, 이영석, 이영림 (2007), 「서양사」, 책세상출판사.

안천(2007), 「타이완의 힘」, 교육과학사.

역사연구모임 (2007), 「단숨에 읽는 세계사」, 베이지북스출판사.

정광균(1999), 「싱가포르 그 나라를 알고 싶다」, 세훈문화사.

한국미국사학회(2006), 「사료로 읽는 미국사」, 궁리출판사.

J.네루지음 최충식, 남궁원 편역 (2008), 「세계사 편력」, 일빛출판사.

Kiss, Bow or Shake hands, How to do Business in Sixty Countries, Teri Morrison, Wayne A. Conway & George A. Border, Ph.D., Adams Media Corporation, Avon, Massachusetts, 1994.

www.wikipedia.com

저자 소개

윤 영 미

현) 수원과학대학교 항공관광과 교수
Fulbright Fellow
2010/2014 평창동계올림픽유치위원회 숙박분과 발제자/위원장
(주)호텔신라 영업기획팀

이화여자대학교 영어영문학 학사
University of Massachusetts, Master of Science
단국대학교 경영학박사

관광실무 영어회화

초판 1쇄 발행	2010년 12월 10일
2판 1쇄 발행	2019년 2월 20일

저 자	윤영미
펴낸이	임 순 재
펴낸곳	**(주)한올출판사**
등 록	제11-403호
주 소	서울시 마포구 모래내로 83(성산동 한올빌딩 3층)
전 화	(02) 376-4298(대표)
팩 스	(02) 302-8073
홈페이지	www.hanol.co.kr
e-메 일	hanol@hanol.co.kr
ISBN	979-11-5685-744-0